Publications on Asia of the
Institute for Comparative and Foreign Area Studies
Number 26

This book is sponsored by the Japan and Korea Program of the Institute for Comparative and Foreign Area Studies (formerly Far Eastern and Russian Institute).

The Development of Realism in the Fiction of Tsubouchi Shōyō

Marleigh Grayer Ryan

UNIVERSITY OF WASHINGTON PRESS
Seattle and London

Printed in the United States of America

Library of Congress Cataloging in Publication Data
Ryan, Marleigh Grayer.
The development of realism in the fiction of Tsubouchi Shōyō.
(Publications on Asia of the Institute for Comparative and Foreign Area Studies; no. 26)
Bibliography: p.
Includes index.
1. Tsubouchi, Shoyo, 1859–1935—Criticism and interpretation. 2. Realism in literature. I. Title.
II. Series: Washington (State). University. Institute for Comparative and Foreign Area Studies. Publications on Asia; no. 26.
PL817.S8Z86 895.6'3'4 75–1451
ISBN 0–295–95382–9

Publications on Asia of the Institute for Comparative and Foreign Area Studies is a continuation of the series formerly entitled Far Eastern and Russian Institute Publications on Asia.

To the memory of my mother

Contents

Acknowledgments

I would like to express my gratitude to the East Asian Institute, Columbia University, for the Research Fellowship under which this study was initiated, and to the Japan Foundation whose funds made possible its completion. Dr. Toyoko Yoshida Ch'en read an earlier manuscript version of this work and made several pertinent suggestions with the special combination of astuteness and sympathy characterizing her treatment of all her students of whom I happily count myself one. Finally my deepest gratitude must go to Professor Roy Andrew Miller who, better than most, knows how to keep the faith.

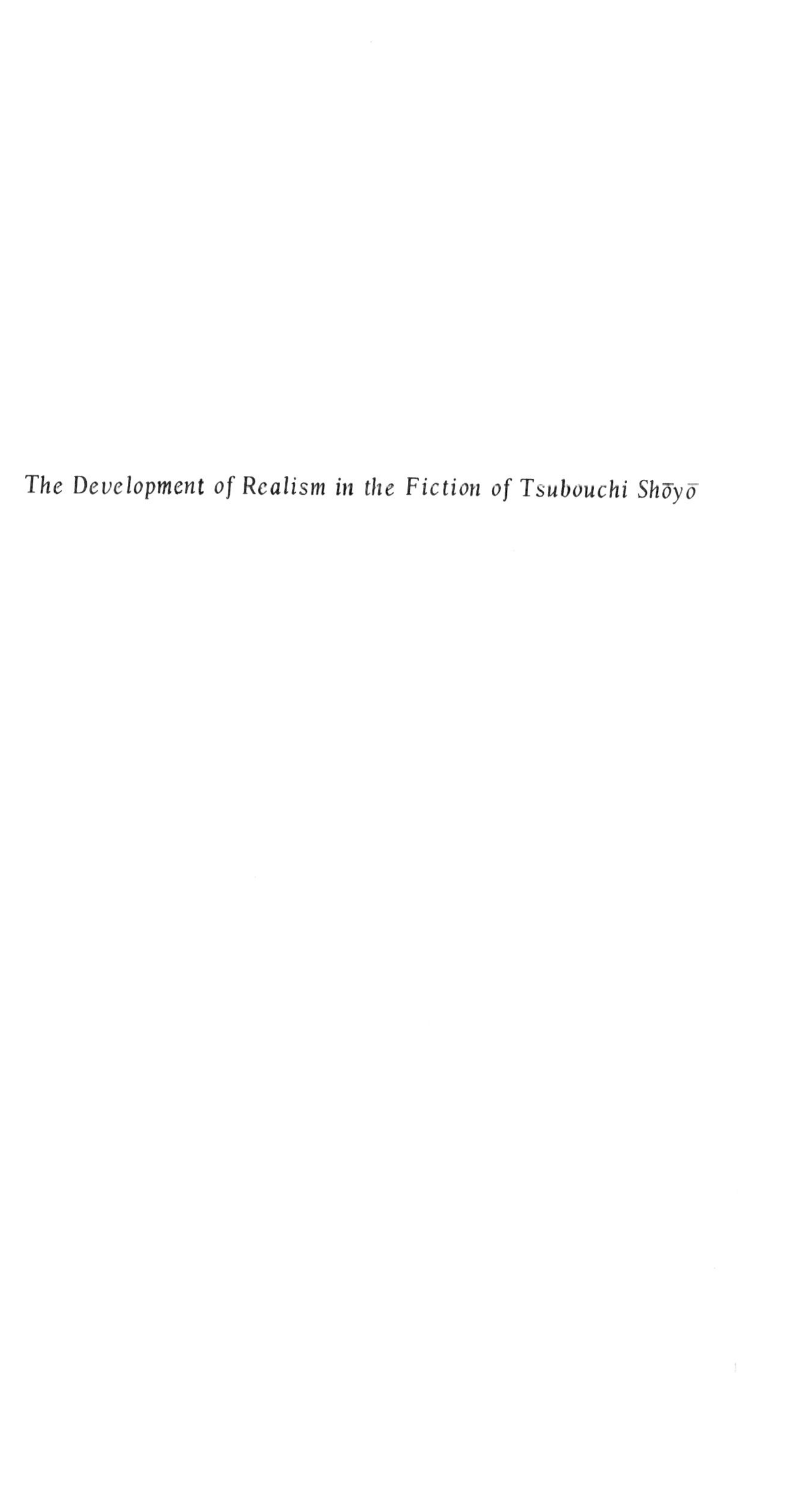

The Development of Realism in the Fiction of Tsubouchi Shōyō

Chapter One

It has been commonplace to say that although there had been a few tentative thrusts at writing realistic fiction in Japan as early as the 1880s, no true realism was produced until the first decade of the twentieth century. Except for recognition of Futabatei Shimei's *Ukigumo* (Drifting Clouds) as the pioneer modern realistic novel, knowledge of the innovations appearing in Japanese literature in the early years of the Meiji period is conspicuously lacking. Both Japanese and Western critics have overlooked the dramatic progress made by writers toward the creation of what was commonly viewed as the "modern" novel. They have concentrated instead on the reactionary tendencies of popular fiction in the last two decades of the century or on ponderous debates between littérateurs over the "meaning" of art and other such tedious topics.

Typically, literary historians have chosen to leap from one outstanding talent to another without adequate consideration of the whole field of literary development. Thus, in analyzing the work of Natsume Sōseki (1867–1916)—whose fame hardly needs to be justified—one scholar recently attributed to him the introduction of psychological realism when, in fact, it had been successfully practiced for more than twenty years before Sōseki started to write, albeit by authors of lesser stature. An enormous amount of attention has also been given to Higuchi Ichiyō (1872–96), who gained a considerable reputation in her own time because she managed to convey some depth of characterization while writing in a style entirely consistent with the fiction of the Tokugawa period. Meanwhile, because critics have been working on the assumption that the literature of the 1880s and 90s was predominantly reactionary, stories with far greater insight into the human condition that fail to reflect marked premodern influence have been ignored.

When the period from 1885 to 1900 is studied in depth, it becomes immediately apparent that there was a continuous development toward modern realistic fiction throughout the period and that the naturalist fiction that overwhelmed the literary world after 1907 was an inevitable result of this development. Despite repeated statements to the contrary, there was, in fact, no major break in this progression. The great popularity of such traditional writers as Ozaki Kōyō (1867–1903) is quite adequately explained by the public's need for a romantic, simplistic literature written in a language with which it was familiar. It does not mean that all of the interest in creating a Japanese counterpart to the English and Russian novels that thousands of Japanese were reading in translation had died or even lay dormant; it simply means that people like Higuchi Ichiyō and Ozaki Kōyō either did not care to or were not able to write it.

In exploring the development of realism in Japanese fiction, it is most appropriate to concentrate on the novels of Tsubouchi Shōyō (1859–1935). He brought into focus the whole question of accurate multidimensional portrayal of characters in a plausible plot structure. His epoch-making essay *Shōsetsu shinzui* (Essence of the Novel) (1885–86) has long been accepted as the most important statement on fiction ever written in Japan,[1] but virtually no attention has been given to his own attempts to implement his theories. When we examine several of his novels carefully, we discover that between 1885 and 1889 Tsubouchi's

[1] For an analysis of this essay and material on his early life and publications, see my *Japan's First Modern Novel*, pp. 37–95.

fiction moved in a continuous line from a wildly uneven, Kabuki-esque first novel that was neither traditional nor modern, Eastern nor Western, to the tight, simple clean tragedy of his last completed work of fiction. From the first we can find evidence of the intelligence and sensitivity that characterizes the best writers of fiction, and taken as a whole, his novels form an almost perfect microcosm of the evolution of realism.

It is this very question of intelligence or, more specifically, intellectuality, that marks the great gulf between writers of traditional and modern fiction in Japan. For a complex of reasons unique to the country and related to the whole social and political fabric of Tokugawa life, writers of fiction in the premodern period tended to be men of limited vision. They were almost completely cut off from the decision-making process in their communities or in the nation at large and could never hope to assume positions of social or political responsibility. From early childhood they were separated from those destined to be the nation's leaders and, while they might brush shoulders with a member of the government at some social event, there could be no question of their rising to power. By and large, artists in the Tokugawa period spent their lives in the area in and around the licensed quarters of the three major cities, Osaka, Edo, and Kyoto. As their art clearly reveals, they knew far more about the lives of geisha and prostitutes, actors and musicians, than about ordinary Japanese of any rank.

The demimonde held a fascination for Japanese people of the Tokugawa not unlike that of Hollywood for Americans in the 1930s and 40s. Fashions were determined by what leading geisha wore and women throughout the country sought to emulate their every gesture. All that was bright, sparkling, and sophisticated in the otherwise rather drab Tokugawa life was thought to emanate from that single source. Thus gossip of the quarter commanded an inordinate amount of attention; many works of fiction were only thinly disguised accounts of the men who spent sizable fortunes in the pursuit of pleasure and the women who were the objects of their attention.

This would never be a literature of the mind. Philosophic lessons to be learned from such fiction were only of the most limited and obvious variety. No food for thought or meditation was presented; the fiction was frivolous, superficial, and completely lacking in significant understanding or insight. The literary forms themselves were repetitive and true innovation was hard to discover. While the fiction was often amusing or diverting, it could never rank as a serious art form.

Much has been made of the negative effect of Confucian and Buddhist precepts in the development of fiction in Japan. Both philosophies decry fabrications and inventions of the mind; Buddhism lists deception as a major sin. In both systems fiction was thought appropriate only as a primer for teaching moral precepts. We consequently find a strong tendency for authors to moralize in works of fiction from medieval times and, in the Tokugawa, even the most licentious story was apt to end with a moral dictum.

The philosophic and religious injunctions against fictionalizing constrained men of substantial rank from even trying their hand at a story and certainly militated against their embarking on a literary career. It relegated fiction to the domain of lesser ranking men, and while writers might enjoy considerable fame in artistic circles, they were still low in the social hierarchy.

Obviously such injunctions alone could never have had so deleterious an effect on the fiction had they not become closely interwoven with other conditions of Tokugawa society. We can find similar ideas in the religious and philosophic precepts of many nations but rarely have they so successfully stultified creativity. A policy of national isolation that banned most books from abroad and a dictatorial government imbued with the notion that art was a potential force for corruption combined with such ideas in Japan to produce a deadening effect. The best minds of the nation did not go into literature; they were directed instead into carrying out hereditary roles in the government. The time spent in creative intellectuality was channeled into that particular combination of philosophic and practical reasoning for which

China and Japan are so well known. It clearly was not spent in practicing and developing the arts.

While men of high rank would not write works of fiction, they and thousands of other Japanese read them. Education of both samurai and commoners increased dramatically in the course of the Tokugawa period and, by the mid-nineteenth century, Japan's rate of literacy appears to have compared favorably with that of Britain and France. Inexpensive books sold in thousands of copies and it is estimated that a single copy of an expensive edition eventually reached ten thousand readers through a complex but efficient system of private lending libraries. Thus we have in the Tokugawa period a true anomaly: a nation with a large active readership producing what by any standard would be considered a truly dismal literature.

The stage was set for a major change and the massive influx of Western ideas in the latter half of the nineteenth century provided that stimulus. Japanese soon learned that the greatest minds of the Western world were deeply concerned with literature in a manner totally alien to their own experience. They discovered that highly respected European philosophers wrote ponderous treatises on its function and meaning. To their total amazement, Japanese found that literature included not only poetry, which from ancient times they too had held in considerable esteem, but fiction as well. The newness, the freshness of this concept to Japanese of the latter nineteenth century is difficult for us to comprehend; for the young men of the time, however, it opened a whole new intellectual world.

The youth that responded with enthusiasm to this innovation were the sons of the hereditary ruling class, the children of the samurai. They would never have become writers of fiction—they would never have even spoken of it seriously—without the influence of the West. They were heirs to the great leadership tradition that excluded the writing of fiction as a career possibility, and their concern with it consequently represented a radical departure from accepted behavior.

While the writing of fiction may not have been part of the samurai heritage, education—its necessity, its dicipline, its personal and national value—had been one of the mainstays of samurai thinking from at least the late eighteenth century. Characteristic of the educational system of traditional Japan was its bilinguality. Youngsters were required to read and memorize works in the Chinese language from a startlingly early age and, throughout their formal schooling, they read and wrote far more in Chinese than in their own language. In adult life, men of the upper classes wrote freely in Chinese; legal records, government documents, personal letters, and diaries were regularly written in Chinese rather than Japanese. No one spoke Chinese, of course, and therefore there existed a long-standing tradition of rapid reading and simultaneous translation from a foreign language.

It required no major change in Japanese thinking, then, for the nation to assimilate the teaching of European languages into the educational system. While they were no doubt unconscious of the reason behind it, the upper classes were entirely receptive to the concept of studying foreign languages precisely because they had been doing so for as long as anyone could possibly remember.

From the early 1870s, school after school introduced some form of instruction in the English language into its curriculum. The texts tended to be of a singularly unliterary flavor; readers in world history designed for American school children were prime favorites. It is obvious that the language was being used from the first as a tool for the acquisition of knowledge to fill the gap created by two hundred and fifty years of isolation. But the boys weaned on such texts soon grew up and entered either a specialized training school or one of the early versions of the modern Japanese universities. There, through foreign languages, they discovered how valued fiction was in the West. Tsubouchi himself describes sessions in his dormitory at Tokyo University in the early 1880s; he tells of how they talked far into the night of Dumas, Dickens, Bulwer-Lytton, and Scott, all by then part of their own life experience. In less than one generation fiction had grown in stature from a form viewed as something between pornography and a cowboy saga to a respected art worthy of serious consideration.

From among these same young men, the graduates of the earliest classes of the modern schools, came those who would write, teach, and criticize literature for several succeeding decades. In 1881 Mori Ōgai, who was to become an outstanding novelist and literary critic, graduated from the forerunner of Tokyo University's medical school with a background in German; Yamada Bimyō, a novelist, grammarian, editor, and lexicographer was in the class behind Ozaki Kōyō at the University Preparatory School from 1884 to 1886; Natsume Sōseki, certainly the most brilliant novelist of the later Meiji period, also entered the same school in 1884 and went on to graduate from Tokyo University in 1893. Tsubouchi's great friend Takada Sanae, who was to emerge as an outstanding educator, head of Waseda University, and advisor to government leaders, graduated from Tokyo University 1882, while Tsubouchi himself finished the course the following year. From the Russian training program of the Tokyo School of Foreign Languages came the novelists Saganoya Omuro and Futabatei Shimei in 1886, both even more thoroughly imbued with the concept of literature as a profoundly serious activity than Tsubouchi. Thus the stage was set for a dramatic change in fiction.

There was no single theory of fiction advocated by these and the many other young men who launched literary careers in the 1880s. Futabatei and Saganoya had been exposed to the somber Hegelian view of Literature as revelatory of the perfect Essence of each moment or each life, and Futabatei, at least, took it very seriously indeed. Ōgai was soon lost in the complex theories of the German romantics. Those who studied English literature—Bimyō, Sanae, and Tsubouchi—seemed much more concerned with the practicalities of novel writing than with any underlying philosophic themes. It is difficult to know how much of this disparity depended on the instruction they received at their various schools and on what they read, and how much on their personal predilections. Ōgai and Futabatei were far more contemplative people than Bimyō and Tsubouchi, and this alone may have been sufficient to produce the marked disparity in their respective approaches to the subject. But philosophic or practical, influenced by Russian, English, or German, they each individually and collectively wanted a new literature for Japan that would be just as valuable as European literature was to Europe.

All seemed to agree that characters in novels had to be people from every walk of life. It would no longer do for fiction to be concerned so exclusively with the demimonde and swashbuckling heroes as it had been in the Tokugawa. To write about ordinary people meant to write about oneself and one's family; the material for plots would come mainly from one's own life experiences. Heroes would be grounded; they would no longer fly off through space to vanquish the enemy or fall under the watchful eye of a guardian spirit as they had throughout the first half of the nineteenth century. The women of the quarter would no longer provide the sole source of romance; ordinary women would, at long last, become subjects suitable for fiction. Domestic problems would dominate as themes, but abstract discussions of ambition, failure, and success would join love and marital questions as sources for literature.

There is disappointingly little discussion of these points in the records of the period; we can only surmise from the novels they wrote what the young men were contemplating. With the exception of reports of Futabatei's ideas in Tsubouchi's memoirs and Tsubouchi's own essay on the novel form, there were few statements on the construction of a novel, characterization, or plot. This is a matter of only limited concern, however, for it is patently obvious that most writers were moving in a similar direction, that is, away from fantasy and toward realism, and away from the closed society of the demimonde into the world at large.

Although the literature of the Tokugawa was frivolous and vapid, it did contain elements that made it relatively easy for Meiji writers to slip into realism. The two dominant forms of theater in the Tokugawa—the Kabuki and the Bunraku (puppet theater)—both used as themes the conflict inherent in an inflexible social structure between romantic love and societal obligation. This conflict was ordinarily expressed in what might be called proto realism. A young man would be trapped in a financial or moral debt that seemingly left him no recourse but suicide with his geisha or prostitute paramour. A warrior would feel called upon to sacrifice his own child to protect the child of his master. Such struggles were at times expressed with considerable depth of emotion and at least some fidelity to life as we might imagine it to be in such a crisis, thus providing a rudimentary kind of realism. Furthermore, the portrayal of male characters as clerks or accountants in the shops of the bustling cities made possible the ready acceptance of everyday human beings as suitable subjects for literary works. Whopping plot flaws and excessive repetition of a few limited ideas prevented Tokugawa plays and fiction from being very convincing; we are constantly aware of the other options open to the benighted heroes or the fallaciousness of their reasoning. The plays and fiction, in short, never developed into realism despite the promising beginning made as early as the first decades of the eighteenth century. They were suggestive of the possibility of realism, however, and certainly facilitated the transition into modern fiction.

There has been, from medieval times, a constant process of cross-fertilization between the various literary arts of Japan, and poetry, fiction, and the theater are far more closely related than they have been in England or France. Playwrights of the Kabuki and Bunraku often used the language and plots of the medieval Nō and each in turn borrowed from the other on occasion. In addition to Kabuki and Bunraku, there was a considerable array of peripheral types of theatrical performance that had their origin in dramatic storytelling and were generally offered with a musical accompaniment. They shared both style and plot with the major theater forms.

Writers of fiction, too, freely borrowed both style and plot from the various types of theater. The very language of fiction was almost inseparable from that of the theater; this diction ultimately derived from classical poetry. In all the literary forms, a rhythmic pattern of 7–5 or 8–6 syllables was favored, creating a style more comparable to English narrative poetry than to prose in any accepted sense. Authors of fiction made considerable use of pillow words, pivot words, puns, metaphors, symbols, and images alluding to classical poetry exactly as did writers for the Nō, Kabuki, and Bunraku.

More subtly, a sense of theater pervaded fiction in the late Tokugawa and early Meiji. Characteristically the fiction was episodic, with static, set scenes and little if any transition from scene to scene. Narrative description or commentary was conspicuously lacking and the plot was conveyed almost entirely through exchanges of dialogue. There was throughout a heightening of emotions; one rarely encounters a character in a state of repose or contemplation. Probably the most extreme examples of this static quality would be the popular works of fiction known by the color of their covers, such as "green book" and "yellow book." These were essentially picture books with the briefest of texts filling in dialogue for necessary continuity. In all there are few devices considered characteristic of the theater that do not occur in traditional Japanese fiction as well and, equally significant, little that might be described as belonging exclusively to the domain of fiction.

In addition to the dominant influence of the theater on Tokugawa fiction, an important infusion of ideas came from China. There was a sudden upsurge of interest in colloquial Chinese in Japan in the latter half of the eighteenth century paralleling a renewal of the study of classical Chinese philosophy. Concern with the Chinese language led to reading colloquial Chinese novels, and by the early nineteenth century we find authors experimenting with Japanese romances modeled on them.

The outstanding practitioner of the genre was Takizawa Bakin (1767–1848) whose long and complex romances commanded a wide audience until well into the twentieth century. He drew upon battles and episodes of heroism from medieval Japanese history to fashion tales not unlike those produced on the Asian mainland; magic, fantasy, and totally improbable events intermingled freely with moments of all-too-human emotion to form an exciting conglomeration. In the late 1880s Bakin was scorned by littérateurs who were offended by his fantastic plots and lack of believable characterization, but the reading public continued to delight in his romances for several succeeding generations.

Bakin's fiction presents an additional difficulty to the modern reader; he wrote in a style so heavily laden with Chinese words and expressions that it frequently reads like a translation from Chinese. The whole rhythm is reminiscent of the special variety of language invented by Japanese people for translating Chinese into their language called *kambun*, and the style used in fiction is therefore known as *kambun-chō*, or *kambun* style. Readers of Bakin would therefore have to be well educated in Chinese for no ordinary training in functional Japanese would enable one to understand his work. As the Japanese educational system changed at the end of the nineteenth century and instruction in Chinese gradually gave way to the study of European languages, the audience for Bakin in the original naturally became smaller. By the early 1870s at least Bakin's stories were being read in simplified versions rather than in the original language he employed. What remained was obviously a far less artistic version of the text, making it even less attractive to Meiji critics than it might otherwise have been.

Writers of the early Meiji felt it was necessary to break with the fiction of the past if they were to create a literature suitable to their time. They did not consider the fiction they inherited worthy of emulation. In part this was an accurate appraisal of the state of Japanese art in the latter half of the nineteenth century. However, it was also symptomatic of their excessive zeal in wanting to escape their heritage and merge as quickly as possible with the civilization of the Western world. They thought of Europe and America—without distinction—as the fountainhead of culture. Seemingly the entire Japanese nation, intellectuals and nonintellectuals alike, came to revere the West in what now appears a most foolish fashion. Amazingly enough, they actually believed the West could provide desirable models in virtually all areas of technology and culture. Furthermore, in many cases, acceptance of Western models precluded continuation of the Japanese tradition. Throughout the last century Japan has undergone several periods of extreme self-rejection, and the 1870s through the 1880s was the first and most dramatic of these.

Modern Japanese fiction, then, was born in an atmosphere uniquely receptive to innovation. It was felt that the past had to be abandoned and something brand new created. In the process much that was important in the Japanese tradition was temporarily lost, but few people at the time were aware of this aspect of the problem. Those who became novelists were among the most forthright in seeking to imitate the West. Indeed the very terms novel and novelist have no true meaning in premodern Japan, for both were products of the period beginning in the 1880s and both were adapted to conform to Western models.

A new literature was possible because for the first time in nine hundred years the field attracted the best young minds of the nation. Once it was understood that in the world at large fiction was produced by highly educated, thoughtful men who commanded universal respect, the writing of novels assumed an entirely new value. It was seen as a vehicle to a position of prestige. The young men who chose to become writers were often descendants of members of the samurai class, but not of the highest ranking or wealthiest families. As was true of other areas of the society, the leading writers came from the stratum just below the top, from families that had held positions of trust and responsibility but never ultimate power in their community or nation. Literature provided an avenue to fame that the hereditary family rank could never have offered. It was a new route to power.

Now, for the first time, literature was to be written for all the people. It was to educate, enlighten, and provide stimulus for personal and national improvement. Entertainment was a secondary consideration; truth, as understood by the philosophers of the West, was to be its goal. This meant a literature that would probe into the hearts of men and make new discoveries, a literature little concerned with outward behavior and profoundly involved with the inner self. It was by no means easy for Japanese writers to make the transition from their own highly superficial fiction to the kind of literature of the mind they found being written in the West, but ultimately they were successful. In part this success was due to the fact that the writers were entirely different by birth, education, and predilection from their predecessors in premodern Japan. In part it succeeded because the nation was ready to slough off the atrocious fiction it had been encumbered with for centuries and assume a new literary stance suitable to an educated, dynamic, world power.

Chapter Two

Tsubouchi is best known in Japan as the first important translator of Shakespeare. Beginning in 1884 he published over the years Shakespeare's complete works, including the sonnets, and his translations of the plays held the stage for more than half a century. In 1935, his final gesture was to call his literary collaborators to his side for assurance that the last translation in a newly revised version of the complete plays would be published in accordance with his specifications. Although they now seem archaic to Japanese people because the language has altered so dramatically since they were written, his translations were clearly the basis for most subsequent versions and are still widely respected. He was also a leader in the movement to create a modern theater in Japan.

Tsubouchi began teaching even before he was graduated from Tokyo University in 1883. He went on to become one of the most important voices in Japanese university life and, through his teaching and publications, was instrumental in founding Japanese literary criticism as it is known today. An impressive number of leading critics of the thirties and forties were his students, and their students in turn are active in the contemporary critical world, teaching in major universities and publishing in considerable volume. They practice an identifiable style of literary criticism that, while perhaps unimaginative to the foreign eye, has a solid, sensible quality characterized by careful research and cautious exposition.

As there was virtually no worthwhile fiction in Tokugawa Japan, neither was there much that can be classified as literary criticism. In a real sense, Tsubouchi invented it for Japan in 1885–86 when his *Shōsetsu shinzui* appeared. Here he employed the tools of Western criticism as he understood them in an attempt to analyze what was wrong with the Japanese fiction of his time, and to suggest ways it could be improved. He seems to have understood Western literary criticism as it was practiced in the latter half of the nineteenth century reasonably well although those elements of Western criticism most strongly dependent on careful reasoning were quite lost on him. Still it is an interesting attempt for its time. Sadly enough it cannot be read with much reward today for it is couched in the language of traditional Japanese exposition and the argumentation is turgid and tedious. Later Tsubouchi was to approach criticism with more objectivity, and therefore with more wit, employing a gentle irony to sidestep the convoluted reasoning of his opponents in literary debates, but in the 1880s he was himself too concerned with the seriousness of his mission to allow his natural good humor to come through. Unlike other Japanese critics, he did not concern himself with philological analysis or with considerations of such details as an author's identity or the dating of a text. He wrote instead about a whole class of literature—fiction—and attempted to define its meaning and function. He used examples of works of fiction from both the East and West, codifying what he considered desirable in a novel. While his conclusions seem excessively moralistic to us today, they appeared highly significant to his contemporaries.

In the *Shōsetsu shinzui*, Tsubouchi spoke of what "ought" to be as if there were some feasible way of determining and maintaining a standard for fiction. He saw clearly that the officially sanctioned Confucian thinking of the Tokugawa had been disastrous for literature, and must have realized that it had often been employed for political rather than moral ends; that is, he must have known that restrictions on the use of politically sensitive material in Kabuki and Bunraku were made to protect the established government and not to keep the public's mind pure. But Tsubouchi did not argue that it was inherently wrong to restrict intellectual activity. Rather he seems to have said that the policies were bad because they were ineffectual and had in fact produced the opposite result from what had been intended. Instead of writing the morally edifying works one presumes the Tokugawa authorities might have favored, authors had invented a whole series of totally transparent devices to permit "acceptance" of the most salacious stories. This was the sort of nonsense Tsubouchi was inveighing against in the strongest terms, not, regrettably, against a whole system of thought that restricted artistic impulse.

Tsubouchi himself might not have understood the implications of intellectual freedom since the first hints of this concept were only beginning to filter into Japanese intellectual life in the 1880s. On the other hand, he must have been quite conscious of how restrictive the Meiji government could be in the political sphere, for he was a supporter of the idea of representative government when that notion was extremely unpopular with the Meiji authorities and was in close contact with the leaders of the movement. He must also have been aware of the official attacks on fiction and the theater made by various government agencies in the 1870s and 1880s. It is difficult to be certain of how he reacted to these problems and even whether he associated them in his mind. Furthermore we do not know for certain whether he considered government intervention in the arts a worrisome thing. Since it would seem that what he disliked most in Japanese fiction was its salaciousness, perhaps he welcomed the official injunctions against sordid plots and vulgar displays in fiction and theater. Their excuse—and in a sense Tsubouchi's as well—was that vulgarity would shock the foreigners now coming to Japan and would harm the image of Japan in the world's eyes. Officially those who dealt with the arts in the Meiji government wanted public performances that would demonstrate how "civilized" Japan was, and they equated civilization with prudery. The famous admonitions to Kabuki performers to correct the historical inaccuracies in their plays introduced in the Tokugawa to get around governmental restrictions, though laudable enough on the surface, were in fact an attempt on the part of the authorities to rid the Kabuki of its more sordid elements and make it presentable as a Japanese national theater.

It will be seen at once how close this was to Tsubouchi's own thinking. In the *Shōsetsu shinzui*, his prose reached its most strident level when he spoke of the need for a new, great literature for Japan, a literature equal to that of the Western world, which he appears to have conceived of as being free of licentiousness. It is this almost Victorian moralizing, this implicit appeal for an uplifting, edifying fiction, that offends the modern reader and makes the *Shōsetsu shinzui* such a museum piece today. He was correct in his negative evaluation of contemporary literature, as the Meiji authorities were no doubt right in saying that much of the contemporary Kabuki was trash, but we are troubled in both instances when we realize what might be sacrificed to obtain the end they envisaged. It is furthermore difficult to credit Tsubouchi with being a bold, original thinker when we consider how much of what he said reflected his own peculiar mixture of Japanese and British prudishness.

As we study several of Tsubouchi's novels in detail, we shall see how encumbered he was by the belief that literature had to "teach," had to define for readers what was "good" or "correct." This attitude was both traditional to Japan and learned from Western books and from the earliest foreigners resident in Japan. Tsubouchi tortured his first two novels with long interpolations on moral and practical issues that nearly destroyed them as works of fiction. His ability to overcome his didactic inclinations and allow life to speak for itself represents the single most important development in his technique as a writer of realistic fiction. This discovery appears not to have been the result of critical reasoning but rather a function of the practicalities of writing a novel. Somehow in the actual process of writing it came to him that to say less—particularly for the author's voice to say less—had far greater impact than to say more. Simultaneously he discovered that the tighter the plot and more limited the number of characters and range of action, the more forceful his message would be.

Tsubouchi was also disappointingly silent on the question of who should write the new literature he described. Although it is clear to the reader that the fiction Tsubouchi wanted to see created in Japan could not be handled by men of limited intelligence and education, Tsubouchi did not make this crucial point. Again we do not know whether he fully realized that profound literature is the work of profound men, or whether perhaps he felt it indiscreet to raise the issue while he was in the process of launching his own literary career. He was, after all, dependent on publishers of the very fiction he was attacking. Furthermore the Japanese literary world was (and still is) extremely close-knit and virtually all writers knew each other, and were socially and financially dependent on each other. It would have taken a brave man indeed to personalize an attack on the contemporary literature with the suggestion that those who were writing it were incapable of anything loftier.

The most important single point made in the *Shōsetsu shinzui* is that fiction should explore beneath the surface and attempt to reveal what makes men behave as they do. Over and over throughout the book Tsubouchi stressed that this is the primary function of literature. This would, of course, make all the difference between a story relating events, no matter how interesting, and a story of profound significance. He argued, too, that the characters of the new fiction should be ordinary men and women, taken from all walks of life, and that what they do should be plausible within the range of actual human behavior.

This then was a many-pronged attack; he was seeking to eliminate fantasy, excessive romanticism, and idealization all at once. It can of course be argued, as Japanese critics have, that the insignificant man as hero had been a stock character in

Tokugawa times and that therefore Tsubouchi was not particularly original. The argument is correct as far as it goes, for in both theater and fiction men of lowly birth and position had appeared, and they were often weak, pathetic creatures easily victimized by society and unable to find adequate solutions to their problems. But Tsubouchi's point was much more profound. He was saying that it is not enough to use ordinary men as heroes, something important must be said about them. At the very least, one must attempt to discover why they are ordinary and what this quality of "ordinariness" means to the way they conduct their lives. This is what psychological penetration is all about, and Tsubouchi understood it well. He himself turned inward to find material for his own fiction. This was an obvious solution to the problem of how to "explore the hearts of men," a phrase he used many times in his criticism to indicate what he felt should be the dominant goal of fiction. While obvious, it was in a sense an ingenious solution, one that Japanese writers of the twentieth century have used over and over, perhaps even to excess.

Japanese society offers a unique problem in the writing of psychological fiction. In the West we have a tradition of articulating our innermost feelings to one another. In most ages, it has been customary for a person to have at least one close friend or sibling to whom innermost secrets were told and, in particularly reticent times, the young have resorted to confessional diaries when no companion could be found to whom they could talk freely. The priest or minister, and today the therapist, often has replaced the friend or relative when the problem has become sufficiently severe, but in all cases we have believed, almost as an article of faith, in the efficacy of articulation.

The exact opposite is the case in Japan. In Japanese society it has been the custom to refrain from telling anyone, at least in words, what is most troubling. It is frequently the case that members of the immediate family will be told nothing in even the most dire emergencies, and certainly they are not told of minor concerns. This verbal restraint has a long history in Japan and is clearly related to the whole system of behavioral ideals codified in the Tokugawa; it has resulted in a nation where to say less is more desirable than to say more. Even on a day-to-day level, it is perfectly apparent to any observer that Japanese people are relatively inarticulate when compared with their Western counterparts. Much is conveyed by hint or suggestion and even by facial expression, but clearly these are far less precise methods of communication than words.

We can easily imagine what a problem this presented to the Meiji novelists trying to emulate the West. Where were the words for intimate conversations to come from? Where were they to find the language of the interior monologue, early recognized as a crucial technique for motivational literature? Of course, Tsubouchi, as a reader and translator of Shakespeare and Dickens, had the best possible models before him, but these models would not easily apply in Japan where writers had habitually announced the most devastating conclusions in a brief line or two, or where the onset of a snowfall, for example, conveyed a whole array of complex thoughts to a theater audience. Tsubouchi struggled with this problem, as did others in the late eighties, until eventually a solution was reached, a solution that involved inventing a new language for expressing ideas never before articulated, and perhaps never before thought.

When Tsubouchi was confronted by the problem of writing about what people thought rather than what they did, he turned inward for his source material, but he did not use his own experiences exclusively. Twentieth-century Japanese fiction has been plagued by a dearth of imagination and novelists have used their own lives as the basis of their novels all too often, but Tsubouchi had other sources and he had the vision to use them. He combined his understanding of himself with his insight into the motivations of other men and, most significantly, into the feelings of women. Here again, a certain limited precedent existed in Tokugawa literature, for women had been the central focus of many plays, particularly women of the licensed quarters, but, as in the case of the male shopkeepers, little of their inner thoughts were convincingly presented.

When searching for a Japanese precedent for the depth of Tsubouchi's female characters, we cannot overlook Lady Murasaki's *Tale of Genji*, for the famous eleventh-century romance was known to him. He and his classmates read aloud from it in the dormitories even in his schooldays, and Tsubouchi had occasion to refer to it in his critical writings. Again, it is uncertain to what degree he understood its broad sweep and magnificence, for little sophisticated literary scholarship had been done on it by then and it is an excruciatingly difficult novel to read, let alone fully comprehend. Tsubouchi spoke of it in the *Shōsetsu shinzui* largely in connection with technicalities of style. It is entirely possible that he recognized and appreciated the scope of Murasaki's portrayal of women, but the depth of his comprehension remains a matter of speculation.

The obvious motivation for his extensive female characterization came from European fiction. He was conversant with the most popular contemporary novelists—Dickens, Dumas, Thackeray, Bulwer-Lytton, among others—and he clearly learned much from them. Furthermore there was something of a feminist movement in Japan in the 1880s, comparable to the contemporary European and American movements. Tokyo was full of talk of education for women, love marriages, and women's "rights," although how well this last term was understood is open to question. Tsubouchi, as a student and teacher, was located at the very hub of many of the new ideas sweeping Japan, and could scarcely have been unaware of the feminist talk. This surely was a factor in his frequent choice of a woman as subject.

At least as significant however was Tsubouchi's own attitude toward women. Although his biographers are only of limited help in this regard, it would seem that some special combination of sensibilities made it possible for Tsubouchi to understand the inner workings of a woman's mind in a most remarkable fashion. Nothing else can explain the way he wrote about women, the characters he created, and the plots he constructed around them. He clearly had the greatest sympathy for disadvantaged women and, even more crucial for his writing, was able to see how the most imposed upon could equally well be kind and generous, or selfish and vicious. His female characters ran the whole gamut from sweet to monstrous, all-giving to totally selfish. As his talents as a novelist grew, so did the subtlety with which he handled his female characters. Thus in his last novel, a very short book over which he labored for months, there is a marvelous dichotomy created by the juxtaposition of a selfish middle-class woman, herself greatly imposed upon by her chauvinist husband, and the docile, trusting little servant girl she misuses in a most offhand way.

This remarkable sensitivity to women invites speculation about Tsubouchi's early life that his biographers have been unable to satisfy. What details we do have contribute to our overall impression of Tsubouchi as having been a uniquely creative member of a diligent but unimaginative family.

Tsubouchi's father was a devoted functionary in the government of the Owari *han*, one of the major provinces in the Tokugawa governmental system. He was in charge of a small community, Ōta, near Nagoya, at the very close of the Tokugawa period. A well-educated, hard working, and deeply religious man, he was greatly concerned with the correct performance of official and familial duties, but certainly was not a man of great imagination. Tsubouchi's maternal relatives, however, boasted at least one poet, and his mother had a great fondness for the theater that she was permitted to indulge on occasion. There is nothing particularly unusual about Tsubouchi's education or inclinations; he learned the Chinese classics by rote as did every boy of his class and read the great adventure tales of Bakin and the stories of other early nineteenth-century writers, first in simplified versions and later in the original. His was a highly literate family, greatly given to reading formally and informally; his father kept records of the books he and his family read, and later Tsubouchi too made a list of all the novels he had read from the lending library in Nagoya. Tsubouchi's early life in Ōta and later in Nagoya where his father took up residence in 1869 was essentially rural, almost rustic in its simplicity and quietude. He was the youngest child and being the last at home when his brothers were already out in the world, was treated almost as an only child by his mother. He was instructed in everything from kendō to archery, and of course in English, for his was an ambitious family, determined on a course of success for each of its several members.[1]

Perhaps the most striking thing about the Tsubouchi family—three boys and three girls reached adulthood—is the ambition they felt, individually and collectively. The family record is one of almost incredible effort to learn, and then to put what is learned to use. They cared greatly for their parents and for each other, and when there was sickness or failure, the weak member was sheltered with loving affection. Such a family is by no means rare in Japan but surely that sort of family background must have had something to do with the man Tsubouchi became: indefatigable in his teaching and writing, critical of his own accomplishments but enthusiastic for the success of others, sensitive and sympathetic in the most profound meaning of those words.

Beyond this, little is to be learned from his early biography. Tsubouchi went to Tokyo in 1876 at the age of seventeen on a scholarship from his home prefecture and eventually became a member of one of the first classes at the newly formed Tokyo University.[2] Very few students attended the university and the

[1] The most valuable source of information on Tsubouchi's early life is *Wakaki Tsubouchi Shōyō* by Yanagida Izumi, which is an attempt at a critical biography. Yanagida, who was a disciple of Tsubouchi, expands considerably on the material in the earlier *Tsubouchi Shōyō*, which he wrote jointly with Kawatake Shigetoshi, but he is still quite careful not to offend Tsubouchi's memory.

[2] The school system was in a continual state of flux throughout the 70s and 80s. The schools Tsubouchi attended in Nagoya and Tokyo changed name and curriculum frequently. Tokyo University itself was quite a rudimentary school while he was in attendance and one has the

public viewed its graduates with considerable awe, but Tsubouchi was quite skeptical regarding its benefits for him.[3] Two of his best known instructors lectured in English—a young literary historian named William Houton and the famous Ernest Fenollosa—but he learned little from either as he did not understand much of what they said. He failed his third year at the university in 1881 and had to repeat the work. As a consequence he lost the prefectural scholarship that had supported him, left the dormitory, and started a small school to earn his living. He also took several jobs as a part-time teacher in private schools around Tokyo. He attributed his failure to the dissolute life he had engaged in with his colleagues; he was finally graduated in 1883, a far more sober man for the experience.

One liaison formed by Tsubouchi in the quarter where he and his friends spent so much of their time proved of great significance to his life and perhaps explains more than anything else how it is he was able to write so well about women. In 1884 he became acquainted with a prostitute named Katō Sen, a young woman six years his junior,[4] and, after continuing to patronize

---

impression that it was more like an English boarding school than a university despite the age of its students.

[3] Tsubouchi describes his university life in "Kai randan," *Shōsetsu shinzui*. In *Meiji bungaku meicho zenshū*, pp. 162–72.

[4] Accurate biographical material concerning Sen is difficult to obtain. The biography of Tsubouchi published by Kawatake Shigetoshi and Yanagida Izumi in 1939 makes only the most formal mention of her, quoting from the entry in Tsubouchi's diary that recorded the date of the wedding, the fact that she had been adopted by a Tokyo family, and the names of those who attended the wedding banquet. After her death, Tsubouchi's nephew and heir, Tsubouchi Shikō—the couple had no children—was prevailed upon to record what he knew of Sen, which he did in 1953 in his *Tsubouchi Shōyō kenkyū* (pp. 31–40). Shikō was most reluctant to tell of her background as we see from the material on pp. 191–92, and left much to be said. Even this limited revelation produced quite a reaction and several articles speculating on this unusual marriage followed. In 1955 Yanagida Izumi wrote briefly of Sen and told how Tsubouchi ceased to visit the quarter after his marriage, adopting a very stern attitude toward sexual indulgences in others (see "Tsubouchi sensei to josei," *Meiji Taishō bungaku kenkyū*, no. 16 [1955], pp. 64–70). Kawatake Shigetoshi published the most revealing

her for three years, arranged for her to move to his house in July of 1886. They were married in October of that year.

The term "prostitute" is used advisedly, for Sen was not a geisha nor did she belong to the higher ranks in the system by which the geisha, courtesans, and prostitutes were arranged in the licensed quarters. The house to which she was bound by contract was the second largest in the Nezu district, a new licensed quarter in downtown Tokyo near the university, established in 1870. Although reputedly beautiful, Sen was not one of the more valued women in the house, being given a third or fourth rank. She had a three-year contract at the house for which she was paid 600 yen.

Sen was apparently born in Nagoya, lived with her mother in Osaka until she was four and then returned to Nagoya to live with relatives until she was in her teens. She then went to live briefly with her mother in Osaka and was soon sold to a house of prostitution in Kobe on a four-year contract. After her contract was paid, she moved on to the Nezu house in Tokyo. By July of 1886 she had paid off half her contract at the house, and with Tsubouchi's promise to repay the balance, she was released from the house and went to live with Tsubouchi. Tsubouchi repaid the debt, as he had paid for his visits to Sen over the years,

---

material in his *Ningen Tsubouchi Shōyō* (1959). In this he tells how he was able to read through a sealed confession left by Tsubouchi. Sen permitted him to read it one long evening in the company of a man named Yamada Seisaku who was a retainer of the Tsubouchis. The document was labeled, in English, "Her past and my several life" (*sic*) and bore the injunction that it should not be opened until after his death. It told of Sen's early years in some detail and made mention of the world's treatment of Tsubouchi as a consequence of the marriage. The next morning Yamada returned the document to Sen, who subsequently destroyed it (pp. 5–27).

Other articles have appeared, but shed little light on the facts. In *Wakaki Tsubouchi Shōyō* Yanagida gives some details of her birth, records again the details of the wedding day, and then appends, as a footnote, the information that she was a prostitute (pp. 194–95). Unfortunately, there are a number of discrepancies between these various reports, and matters such as Sen's date of birth and age at the time they met remain in some doubt.

with his own earnings. His father had died in 1882 and his older brothers soon after, but Tsubouchi had refused his inheritance and insisted on being completely self-supporting. There were times, however, when he had to resort to usurers to maintain the expenses associated with Sen, for these were huge sums in those days.

Sen arrived at Tsubouchi's house, which functioned as a dormitory for a group of resident students, by rickshaw one July afternoon, accompanied by her possessions in a wicker basket. The boys were startled and soon there was much gossip about the young woman in Tsubouchi's house. A wealthy friend strongly advised Tsubouchi to have a proper wedding ceremony. This gentleman, a banker, arranged for Sen to be adopted by one of his employees, thus giving her the proper air of respectability. The wedding took place in October 1886.

Sen was never accepted by Tsubouchi's family and never, in a sense, by society at large. Little is known of her in the years after the marriage. Tsubouchi confessed that he gave up his original plans to educate her and instead had a cooking teacher come to the house. In addition to cooking, Sen also apparently enjoyed gardening a great deal. In his final secret testament relating the details of their meeting and marriage, Tsubouchi revealed how valuable she had been to him in managing the family's finances, a task for which she had considerable talent. Those who knew her as his wife report that she was restrained and reserved, giving the impression of a completely respectable woman. There is no question, however, that Tsubouchi's career as an educator was hindered by his marriage. He was forced to resign a position as principal of Waseda Middle School after gossip appeared in the newspaper and, fearing a scandal, he subsequently declined nominations to several posts and honors for which he would have been the most appropriate choice.

One extremely interesting fictional document relating to Tsubouchi's marriage to Sen remains. Between November of 1885 and August of 1886, Tsubouchi was writing a novel entitled *Imotose kagami* (A Mirror of Marriage), which tells the story of a well-educated middle-class man who marries an illiterate fishmonger's daughter. In this novel, written in the months before he married Sen but after he had been involved with her for two years, he described the dreadful mistakes made by a man much like himself in forming such an unsuitable marriage on a romantic impulse. Lacking information from the author or his contemporaries, we are entirely at a loss to do other than speculate about the relation between this hero and Tsubouchi. It is far too tantalizing a question to leave untouched—although here again the Japanese critical world has made only the barest mention of a possible association—for it would have been impossible for him to conceive and execute such a plot without seeing how similar it was to the life on which he himself was about to embark. The book is filled with comments about how foolish the hero was to have married the girl and how unfortunate it is when a man is free to make his own choices instead of being guided by the wisdom of his parents. The voice of the author appears to be on the side of reason and restraint, and against the actions of the hero, but once we realize how closely Tsubouchi's life parallels the plot we must assume the voice of the author here is more of a fictitious character than is the hero. The novel is a very serious study of the personality of the hero and it certainly assumes greater dimension when we understand the author's personal connection with the plot.[5]

[5] Very little has been written about this extremely interesting novel. One short study of it makes the association between Tsubouchi's own life and the story but fails to develop the idea to any degree, Wada Shigejirō, "Shōyō *Imotose kagami* shiron," *Ritsumeikan bungaku* (January 1958), pp. 1–13.

Chapter Three

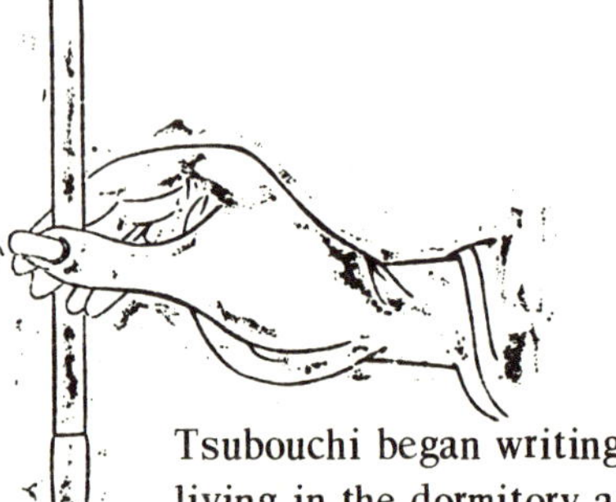

Tsubouchi began writing fiction when he was still living in the dormitory as a student.[1] Between 1885 and 1889 an impressive array of his fiction was published, including several political allegories. For the purposes of examining how he developed into a writer of realism, we shall study four of his novels in considerable detail. Each plot will be described at length, its strengths and weaknesses will be analyzed, and each will be examined to try to determine how it reflected his growth as an artist. A summary of contemporary reaction to each of the books will also be attempted, for no work falls completely on deaf ears, and a true measure of a writer's worth is surely related to how his contemporaries valued him.

The first and most famous of his novels is *Tōsei shosei katagi* (The Character of Present Day Students), which he started writing in a great flush of enthusiasm on April 9, 1885.[2] It began

[1] A pleasant insight into his writing habits as a student is afforded by his school friend Ichijima Shunjō in "Meiji bungaku shoki no tsuioku," *Shōsetsu shinzui*. In *Meiji bungaku meicho zenshū*.

[2] In June 1884 he contracted to do a novel to be called *Yūgaku hachishonen* (Eight Young Traveling Students). Little was written but Yanagida believes that material from this abortive attempt was used the following year in *Tōsei shosei katagi* (*Wakaki Tsubouchi Shōyō*, pp. 142–43).

to reach the public on June 24th. The novel was published in sections in paper bindings resembling pamphlets, first chapter by chapter, then, from the tenth chapter on, two chapters at a time. In March of 1886 it appeared as a complete book in twenty chapters; many other editions followed.

It was an enormous commercial success and made Tsubouchi's reputation as a writer. Its success can be attributed at least in part to the similarity it bore to Japanese fiction with which the public was already familiar. As the title indicates, it shares some of the qualities of what is known as *katagi mono* or character sketches. These were loosely organized fictional portraits drawn around a central theme. Each sketch was generally limited to the length of a short vignette, and books were composed of groups of sketches under such general classifications as worldly young men or retired old men, courtesans or concubines, maidservants or mothers-in-law. Most were very humorous and not intended to convey any serious message. Far too casual to be anything but superficial, they gave pleasure through their slapstick humor and suggestiveness. *Tōsei shosei katagi* promised to be such a delightful revelation of a new and fascinating social group, the modern university student. Readers were tantalized at the idea of gaining an inside glimpse into the mischief practiced by this new elite.

Tōsei shosei katagi does indeed contain a good deal of frivolity but it also has a very complex plot. Although unraveling the plot alone may well occupy a reader's full attention, there are several interesting characters developed, and Tsubouchi's skill in handling this vast array of personalities and events is itself fascinating.

This novel has been much maligned in the twentieth century; one recent article refers to it as an "atrocious" novel. Tsubouchi has contributed to this evaluation by frequently deprecating this, his first novel, as the indulgent work of a foolish youth. There is no question that it fails to conform to any twentieth-century Western concept of a well-structured novel, but it has a dimension of its own and must certainly be studied on those terms.

It is a massive work, attempting to encompass within its pages the whole spectrum of student life in the early 1880s. In its size and scope it has few precedents in all of Japanese fiction. Despite the title and the author's desire to write of student life as he knew it, the main plot actually concerns the origins of a geisha named Tanoji whose true parentage is not revealed to her or to the reader until the last chapter. In the end we discover that she is actually the daughter of a respectable family. Another girl tries to trick Tanoji's family into believing she is their daughter, but eventually Tanoji is returned to her rightful parents. Her life is interwoven, directly and indirectly, with those of a considerable number of men and women, each of whom is in turn developed as a character in the novel.

In the course of the novel we learn that Tanoji had been lost to her family during the Ueno War of 1868. Her mother had been shot while attempting to carry Tanoji to safety through embattled city streets. As she fell, she tripped over the kneeling figure of another woman who had stopped to adjust the cords that held her own child on her back. Tanoji fell from her mother's arms and the other child tumbled from her mother's back. In struggling to her feet, the other woman had scooped up Tanoji by mistake and rushed off to catch up with the man who was leading her. Tanoji's mother died a few moments later, the strange child by her side. The other woman, on realizing she had made the error a short time later, decided to abandon Tanoji in a doorway after first removing a golden amulet case containing money and the child's identification.

Tanoji was discovered by a poor but kind old woman who, taking her to be the illegitimate child of good parents, cared for Tanoji until her own death. The woman's adopted son proved to be unscrupulous and Tanoji, by then ten years old, was sent off by herself in search of Gensaku, a brother of the old woman. On the road she met Komachida Kōji, a petty bureaucrat lacking in thrift, his mistress Otsune, an ex-geisha, and Kōji's son Sanji, then thirteen years old. They listened to her story sympathetically and upon discovering that Gensaku was in no position to care for the girl, took her into their family. A few years later, Kōji[3] fell badly into debt and Otsune went back to being a geisha. She was quite successful and when Kōji's official wife died, she took the girl with her. As a successful geisha, Otsune was able to help Kōji financially. Despite the fact that he was taking money from a geisha, Kōji asked the girl Tanoji not to visit his household as people would think he had sold her to pay his debts. Kōji eventually recovered his position and Sanji resumed his studies.

The other little girl abandoned on the battlefield had been rescued by a young man, Mizuno Teishichi, who was anxious to flee Tokyo to escape his debtors. He picked her up from the arms of Tanoji's mother and carried her off to his home province. His only clue to her parentage was a dagger he took from Tanoji's dead mother whom he of course imagined to be the mother of the child he was rescuing. A man of good intentions but singular ill-fortune, he eventually ended up in Tokyo again, forced to sell the girl into prostitution. She took the professional name of Kaodori. Teishichi died soon after, still penniless, and the girl was left alone in the world with only the vaguest hope of ever finding her real family. She too of course believes there is some connection between the dagger and her family.

This generally is the background of the story that we learn through a series of flashbacks and other devices early in the novel. At the actual time of the action of the novel, we find that soon after becoming a prostitute Kaodori meets a student named Moriyama Tomoyoshi and realizes that the crest on his *haori* jacket is the same as the one on her dagger hilt. She asks him about the crest but is too embarrassed to suggest any connection between herself and his family. On being questioned, she tells him that her mother had been lost in the Ueno War and that she had been raised by her father. Tomoyoshi had lost his mother and

[3] It is interesting to note that in the original text Tsubouchi refers to the male characters by their family names and the female characters by their given names. He continued this practice in all his novels.

sister in that uprising; his father had searched for them over the years. It passes his mind that this girl may possibly be his sister and he does not stay the night with her. After much inner debate, he decides not to tell his father of this encounter or to pursue the matter further with the girl; he convinces himself that such easy solutions do not occur in real life.

Nothing more comes of this until many months later when a friend of Tomoyoshi, Kurase Rensaku, goes to the house where Kaodori works wearing Tomoyoshi's *haori* with the recognizable family crest. Kaodori tells him all she knows of her background, adding that the crests match, and giving him a letter for his friend. Kurase finally gives the letter to Tomoyoshi four months later when he goes to return the *haori* and some money he had borrowed. He relates all Kaodori told him of her history.

Kaodori also tells an older prostitute named Ohide about the crests. Ohide, who has been working in the same house for some months, is Kaodori's real mother. She produces the gold amulet bag that contained Tanoji's identification and persuades Kaodori to use the dagger and amulet bag to convince the Moriyama family that she is their daughter. They would then buy her freedom from prostitution and she would be able to start a new life even if the truth were later discovered.

At the time of the Ueno War, Ohide had been the concubine of a merchant named Miyoshi Shōemon, who is coincidentally a relative of the Moriyamas. Her lover, a dissolute fellow named Zenjirō, is the father of Kaodori (though Miyoshi believed her to be his own child). Zenjirō thought to use the confusion of the uprising to remove Ohide and Kaodori from Miyoshi's house; they thus found themselves in the midst of the battle. While making their way across Tokyo, Zenjirō was killed and Ohide knocked down. It was then that Kaodori slipped from her back and the mixup of the children occurred.

Zenjirō had a younger sister and she turns out to be Otsune, the geisha who became Komachida Kōji's mistress and Tanoji's protector. Otsune knew that Zenjirō had fathered Ohide's child and had kept track of Ohide's whereabouts over the years. By the end of the novel, Otsune has been taken in by a man named Sonoda, a younger employee of Miyoshi, and is about to become Sonoda's official wife. Miyoshi has by then become a wealthy banker; he has rented his house to Sonoda and it is here that the climax of the novel takes place. The elder Moriyama, Tomosada, has had a dream about his lost child, as he frequently had in the past, and has once again advertised for news of her in the newspaper. The advertisement gives Otsune's name as a reference. Ohide seizes the opportunity to present Kaodori as the Moriyamas' daughter. Tomosada is at hand to hear her story and accepts Kaodori as his child.

As Ohide talks with Otsune and Tomosada, his son Tomoyoshi is hiding in an adjoining room with his friend Kurase. Tomoyoshi realized that while Kaodori had told Kurase of the dagger when they first met, she had made no mention at that time of the amulet bag, and therefore something must be wrong with her story now, for she presents the amulet bag along with the dagger as evidence of her heritage. Miyoshi Shōemon then comes in and confronts Ohide, demanding to know what has become of the child she took from his home. Miyoshi too has followed the course of Ohide's unsavory career, awaiting some clue to the whereabouts of the child before approaching her. He had overheard her plotting with Kaodori and followed her to Sonoda's house.

Old Gensaku, the brother of the woman who had raised Tanoji, is also involved in Ohide's plot. He works at the same house as Ohide and Kaodori, and hears them plotting to trick the Moriyamas. He challenges Ohide with the story of Tanoji, which he had learned from his sister, and they realize that she must be the child Ohide picked up by mistake and later abandoned. But Gensaku had lost contact with Tanoji after his sister's death and believed her dead. He allows Ohide to buy his silence and becomes a coconspirator in the plot. Just as Ohide and Kaodori are on their way to the Sonoda house in response to the advertisement, however, Gensaku hears of Tanoji's whereabouts and rushes off to see her, confessing all.

As Miyoshi is questioning Ohide about the lost child, Tomoyoshi steps forward with Tanoji and Gensaku, and the whole tale unravels. Although Kaodori is thus revealed as Ohide's child by Zenjirō, her connection with Miyoshi and relation to Otsune cause them to give her a settlement that would presumably enable her to buy her way out of prostitution.

Running through the novel is still another plot line. Komachida Sanji, the son of the man who took in Tanoji as a child, realizes he is in love with her when he meets her after a long separation. A relatively sober and conscientious student, his contact with her causes considerable damage to his reputation. One of her admirers is a young lawyer named Yoshizumi Kiyoshi whose brother teaches at the University. Sanji is finally suspended from school, and, after a period of reflection in his father's house, resolves to break with Tanoji and pursue his studies seriously again. When Tanoji's true parentage is discovered, Tomoyoshi and Kurase, who are close friends of Sanji's, rush off to tell Sanji the good news.

* * * * * * *

It is apparent then that the novel is at least as much concerned with the lives of geisha and prostitutes as it is with students. This was, as we have noted, in keeping with a well-established tradition in Japanese letters and assured the novel popular success. Looking back on the literature of the Tokugawa and early Meiji, it is as if virtually nothing interesting happened to women who did not reside in the few square miles encompassed by the licensed quarter of Japan's major cities. Merchants' daughters and even young women of the samurai class—provided they were immoral enough—occasionally received a writer's attention and there were, of course, those silently suffering wives of the young men who squandered all in pursuit of emotional satisfaction. But by and large the world of the imagination, both theatrical and fictional, was inhabited by women who were not bound by the restrictive conventions of normal Japanese life. Romance was a proper subject for fiction but had little to do with marriage or indeed with the lives of respectable young women at all.

Tsubouchi's personal experience with women was almost exclusively in the licensed quarter. As we have seen he had frequented the quarter since his university days and had obviously learned a great deal about the life there that, added to the knowledge he gained through earlier Japanese literature, provided the background for his book. Even if he had decided to break with convention and write about ordinary women, it is doubtful that Tsubouchi would have known what to say. Since leaving his family in Nagoya in 1876 at the age of 17 and going to Tokyo to study, Tsubouchi had lived entirely in the company of men. Even his earlier education had been in boys' schools. His understanding of women therefore was limited to his recollections of his mother and sisters, and would hardly have any relevance to the creation of a romantic novel. Moreover his sympathies lay with the women of the quarter whom he considered unfortunate victims of fate. In a later novel he mentions that it is the European practice to look down in scorn on such women while it was the Japanese way to pity them; his was clearly the way of his own countrymen. He was of course deeply involved with Sen by the time he wrote this novel and would have learned much from her.

Given the limitations of the fictional form in which he chose to work, Tsubouchi manages to convey a good deal about his characters. Continuing methods long accepted in Japanese fiction and drama, he links his enormously complicated plot together with a medley of direct action, flashbacks, and reportage. Dialogue tends to be limited, but evocative, and we find we know the characters better than we might have expected. As we shall see below, there are instances when the system breaks down with almost laughable results, but on the whole Tsubouchi does a creditable job.

Tanoji, about whom so much of the plot revolves, never assumes the proportions of the European heroines Tsubouchi admired—Nina of *Rienzi*, for example, a novel mentioned several times in *Tōsei shosei katagi.*[4] But within the Japanese context she is not at all poorly drawn. We encounter her in the first chapter as a young geisha, deferential to the older woman Benkichi, whom she accompanies, coy and witty with her customers. Soon she meets Sanji, by chance, and must hurriedly convey her pleasure at seeing him after a long separation and her desire to speak with him at greater length. Her customers are waiting, already thoroughly intoxicated, and to delay would be to incur their displeasure and very likely injure Sanji's reputation as well. What she says is not unusual or profound, but it is appropriate to putting across this complex of ideas. We feel her discomfort and humility. We learn that the man she refers to as father, Komachida Kōji, does not want her to see Sanji. It is also clear that Sanji is attracted by her new-found glamour. The entire exchange occupies no more than a few lines and yet, were we to reflect upon it, we could probably fill in many of the details spelled out in subsequent chapters. The seeds of almost all the elements of the plot and many of the important characters are here: the mysterious sister who is not a real sister; the serious student drawn to the demimonde; the jealous rival Yoshizumi, one of Tanoji's customers; the other men, Miyoshi and Sonoda, who reappear in the final chapters to put the pieces of the puzzle together. And we realize, significantly, from this first chapter that the plot will be more important than any of the characters.

The history of the Komachidas' connection with Tanoji occupies the fourth and fifth chapters of the novel. It is written as a narrative, the author explains parenthetically, although Sanji is meant to be telling it directly to his friend Moriyama Tomoyoshi. When the Komachidas meet Tanoji she is a child of either seven or ten, depending upon which page one is reading,[5] and has been

[4] Tsubouchi had published a free translation of about half of Bulwer-Lytton's novel in 1884. For a discussion see my *Japan's First Modern Novel*, pp. 49–51.

[5] We cannot make too much of Tsubouchi's failure to keep the age of his characters straight. The problem is endemic in Japanese fiction. It is clearly related to the vague system for calculating people's age in Japan and, even further, to the confused system of counting

raised by the laundress at whose door she had been deposited. And yet, amusingly enough, she speaks in the most elegant Japanese as if she were from an aristocratic family. The Komachidas are surprised at her good manners and speech, as well they might be. This bit of inappropriateness rivals the foolishness of the statement that the laundress assumed the child she found to be of good parentage although she was not well dressed and had no identification. We may be dealing here with the author's own acceptance of a traditional aristocratic bias—that birth will tell—or his use of that belief, which is widely held in Japan, for the purpose of moving his plot along through some of its knottier moments. In either case, it does not enhance the credibility of the novel for the discriminating reader.

The point does, however, establish that Tanoji[6] is no ordinary person and that she will eventually be connected to a good family. It makes her romantic liaison with Sanji more acceptable; we feel confident that they will eventually be able to get together.

There is only one scene in which Tanoji speaks at some length. In chapter thirteen, she and Sanji are brought together in Otsune's house after not seeing each other for more than a month.[7] They are both bitter over having been insulted by Yoshizumi and the older geisha Benkichi in an encounter the reader hears about at second hand. They want revenge but are fearful of the consequences of a direct confrontation on Sanji's

years. Similarly, we cannot be certain of the true age of the children who were mixed up in the original exchange. The age is given as three but may, in fact, be anywhere from one to three.

6 Her childhood name is Oyoshi. The women all have several names since it is the custom for entertainers to take professional names when they assume certain levels of competency. This adds even greater confusion to the various lines of the plot, although obviously more for the foreigner than for the Japanese reader who accepts such things with ease.

7 No exact time is given. Sanji is out of school for four weeks but we have no way of knowing how much time elapsed between the evening of his encounter with Yoshizumi and his suspension from school, nor from the day he returned to school until this meeting.

already bleak reputation. Sanji tries to persuade Tanoji that she would be better off with someone else, and offers a series of excuses for being unable to continue their relationship. Tanoji tells him that she has been ill over not hearing from him; she is determined to wait no matter how long it takes for his career to be established. She has even been equipping herself to be his wife someday by reading and practicing needlework. Behind Sanji's cold analysis of their future prospects lies his conviction that being a geisha she is unsuitable as a wife for a man concerned about his social reputation. In response, she mentions a celebrated contemporary story of a geisha who eventually made a respectable marriage. Sanji remains unmoved.

Tanoji does not suggest that his father's disapproval is indeed peculiar when one considers that she became a geisha because of Kōji's inability to support her, or that Kōji had kept Otsune, a former geisha, for many years. Surely the system of mutual obligation and responsibility is breaking down here somewhere, but neither Tanoji nor anyone else in the novel is concerned about it.

In other ways as well Tanoji shows considerable delicacy in dealing with the complexities of her relationship with the Komachidas. In this scene she indicates that she has hesitated to write to Sanji at school for fear of further implicating him in her life; neither could she bring herself to go to his home. Concerned that illness might account for his protracted silence, she finally addressed a letter to the school, which Kurase, who seems to have a propensity for holding on to things, kept for Sanji. Even after reading the letter, her lover did not contact her; they are meeting here only because of Otsune's intervention. Tanoji is hurt and perhaps somewhat angry, but is willing to accept all this if only Sanji will be hers someday.

This is assuredly naïve of her and exceedingly romantic—a point that, we learn from the author's asides, worried Tsubouchi himself—but it does reflect her spirit. She tells Sanji quite clearly that she thinks he has treated her rather shabbily but she is not going to give up easily. She shows here the same stubborn strength she demonstrated when Yoshizumi insulted them earlier. Unable to retort directly to Yoshizumi, a patron, she was driven to a bitter exchange with the geisha Benkichi, and put a stop to the quarrel by declaring her love for Sanji and dragging him off. Despite the secondhand reporting of the earlier scene, Tanoji's strength of personality stands out and is consistent with her romantic view of life.

This is their final encounter in the novel. As the last chapter ends, the characters are celebrating the happy outcome of the various mysteries and we can assume that they eventually marry. If one is to take it at all seriously, it is difficult to speak of Tanoji's melodramatic life without considering the complicated morality it demonstrates. At seventeen—which might, of course, mean fifteen or sixteen—she is a geisha of some experience. It is obvious from the tone of the novel that then, as now, a geisha was considered superior to a prostitute, but still not a person ambitious men often marry, although there were a few celebrated cases in the Meiji period. There is considerable discussion of this point, not only between Sanji and Tanoji, but also among several of Sanji's friends. It would appear that she is immediately acceptable however once her bloodline is established and all consideration of her past life is abruptly forgotten. We must recognize, too, that Tsubouchi may be working out some of his own thoughts in this novel. He may have already begun contemplating what it would be like to marry Sen, and was here reflecting his hope that it would all prove somehow to be simple.

Of the students, we have the greatest understanding of Sanji and Tomoyoshi. Both are well integrated into the main plot line and are seen in enough diverse situations to gain considerable dimension. They are not simple to analyze, and yet their very complexity lends a degree of authenticity.

We never see Sanji with Tanoji when they are happy; we must accept the reports of the affair we receive, often most casually, from the other characters. Some mention is made of them by virtually all the students but few explore the matter in any depth. Since Sanji is almost always unhappy or defensive when he appears, we have a rather negative impression of him. But as the hero and the object of Tanoji's love, we can assume he is an attractive and pleasant enough fellow under normal circumstances. His intelligence as a student is attested to on several occasions, including parenthetical notes by the author. His conversation lacks the vulgarities indulged in by some of the other students, and he shows a commendable sobriety when defending his decision to obey his father's wishes to stop seeing Tanoji.

Sanji does, however, tend to be stuffy and pompous. He often assumes an affected, sophomoric moral tone. In chapter eleven, he is walking along a busy street with Kurase. Sanji is looking pale and sickly, and Kurase expresses his concern for Sanji's well-being. He tries to persuade Sanji to go carousing with him. Sanji hesitates; Kurase mocks his new-found virtue and hints that he is thinking too much about Tanoji.

> Komachida: You talk like a fool. I'm a man. Once I make up my mind, it's made up. Of course she wrote me but I never even answered her. She's a mere woman; she's had all sorts of problems so she writes me like that. 'Frailty thy name is woman!'[8] You can't rely on them. You probably think I'm depressed because I've got her on my mind. You misunderstand the situation completely. I don't know whether I'll be able to do it, but I promised myself long ago 'to be something.' Should I ruin my life for the sake of a woman? Unfortunately I'm too much of an idealist. Sometimes I dream up some wild scheme 'fallaciously' and try to impose Western ideas on Japanese society. That's where I make my mistake. But I'm not the only one; all of Japan is like that. You are like that too. You just cited *Rienzi*. How can that be a good example for real life? Burning with ambition, Rienzi bolstered

[8] Single quotes here indicate expressions given in English in the text. The author accompanies the English with a reading for pronunciation in the Japanese syllabary and follows it with a parenthetical definition.

> up his courage with the help of a woman and finally succeeded. Isn't that a 'weak' story? Lytton, through his great talent, exposed the depths of human emotions. It's not praiseworthy. It may not be important if it doesn't affect your future but with women all sorts of unexpected complications come up. If you don't escape the bonds of love, you will have endless difficulties. For example, depending on the time and place, you will surely have 'pecuniary' worries; 'physical assistance' is necessary. At the same time, you are in all likelihood envied by some and despised by others. As long as you're emotional you're apt to get into fights because of your pride. This all comes about because you're involved in sex; if you look for the real cause, it all goes back to women. Someone once said that if you search to the root of anything you find a woman. Women really are frightening. After you're established in life, you may have some freedom of movement but while you're a student, not yet settled in your own home, you can't afford to waste your precious time or let yourself be distracted. And so you have to say women are terribly 'dangerous' unless you're an awfully unusual person. And if you add in politics and all, it's both dangerous and unprofitable. Because if you still choose to go ahead and play around, you'll be diverted from a scholar's true purpose, which is to direct the course of public opinion. While it's true for someone going into politics, how much more is sex. . . .[9]

Kurase cuts him off here and suggests that his argument is out of line with the realities of the situation. He cannot understand why Sanji does not continue to see Tanoji from time to time.

Here we see Sanji in his least attractive pose; the young Meiji man out to lead his nation, and incidentally himself, to

[9] *Tōsei shosei katagi, Shōyō senshū,* Bessatsu 1, pp. 153–55.

greater things. In response to a criticism of another point—that the students were too vulgar—Tsubouchi defended his novel as a true picture of the way students behaved in the period 1881–82.[10] Setting the novel in that year establishes the chronology as being contemporaneous with the author's own life, and makes Sanji and his friends the same age Tsubouchi would have been at that time. Which, if any, of the characters Tsubouchi most strongly identified with is not easy to determine, but there is some reason to believe that the romance between Sanji and Tanoji was suggested by events in the life of Tsubouchi's school friend Takada Sanae and a girl related to the owner of a tempura bar they frequented. Furthermore we cannot overlook the similarity to events in Tsubouchi's own life. Tsubouchi has denied that there were any real models for the individual characters and maintained that he was only trying to show life as it was in a Tokyo University dormitory at that time.[11] No doubt this is true, but we cannot avoid feeling that he must have heard such theorizing as Sanji's many times, perhaps even from his own lips.

At several points in the novel Tsubouchi remarks on the injustice with which women are treated in romantic affairs and specifically refers to Tanoji as the victim of a "romantic ideal." We can take this to mean that the author saw her devotion to Sanji as wasted and did not admire Sanji's treatment of her. He does not disparage personal ambition; indeed he opens chapter nine with a strong affirmation of its value. He seems to be saying then that Sanji is an intelligent and perceptive man but one who is very much the victim of conflicting emotions. Sanji does not know what he wants most in life and in the process of trying to discover his proper course is trampling on people almost too casually. A very human kind of hero indeed.

Moriyama Tomoyoshi is more intelligent and reasonable than

[10] The criticism appeared in the new books column of the *Jiji shimpō* November 18, 1885, and is reprinted in Kōjiro Tanesuke, "*Tōsei shosei katagi* kaidai," p. 8.

[11] Kawatake Shigetoshi and Yanagida Izumi, *Tsubouchi Shōyō*, pp. 94–95, 142–43. For further information concerning Takada see my *Japan's First Modern Novel*, pp. 41 ff.

Sanji but he too engages in some convoluted thinking. Although it occurs to him that the prostitute Kaodori might be his long lost sister, he does not investigate the matter or, even more incredibly, mention it to his father. His reasoning: mysteries so long unsolved cannot be solved so simply. Furthermore, he does not care to admit to his father how he met her. He decides to wait three or four years to look into the matter further!

This remarkable conclusion is made even more startling by his later defense of Sanji's decision to give up Tanoji on the grounds that marriage to a geisha would be detrimental to his career. What then of Kaodori, living the life of a prostitute for three or four years until he gets around to seeing if she is his sister? Inasmuch as Tomoyoshi is referred to by both the author and several of the other characters as intelligent, sober, and sensible, we can only assume that he has had a singular lapse of good sense or that Tsubouchi had trouble working this into the plot. It obviously worried the author since Tomoyoshi belabors the point with discussions of how he must not fall victim to "romantic idealism" and how such coincidences happen only in fiction. Was Tsubouchi here too thinking of Sen, whose contract at the house still had one year to run? If he loved her as much as it seems, he must have been himself hard pressed to find rationalizations for leaving her in Nezu for the term of her contract (even if it would have been next to impossible to raise the money for her release).

Tomoyoshi is teaching law in a private academy while finishing his training at the University. In the course of the novel he opens a law office, grows a mustache and Vandyke, and embarks on a successful career. He is both admired and envied by the other students and is, on the whole, more likable than Sanji. Genuinely concerned for Sanji's welfare, he tries to offer him good, practical advice. He is fond of his father and they appear to have a sound relationship, although he speaks of him as "old-fashioned" and "dull," an attitude far more shocking in Japan than in the West. Like Sanji, he is a rounded human being with a memorable personality.

Kurase Rensaku, too, although not as important to the plot line, comes through to the reader as a believable character. More direct and impetuous than the other two, he blunders along trying to help the course of romance here and there with a creditable warmth.

It would seem that the other students appear almost solely for comic relief in the tradition of the *katagi mono*. Sugawa Teizaburō and Miyaga Tadashi spend a good deal of time in the licensed quarter. Early in the novel (chapter two) Sugawa is literally dragged into a house of prostitution where he meets a girl of fourteen or so named Otoyo. This incident, from which he has considerable difficulty extricating himself, is the start of a protracted relationship with Otoyo. His evenings in the gay quarter are costly to his pocket and his reputation, and he gets into various ridiculous situations because of them. While Miyaga figures in several scenes, there is little to distinguish him as a character.

Ninna Tōichi is one of the more serious students. Like his classmate Tomoyoshi, he can be logical and detached in an argument. His departure for study in England is the occasion for a farewell party around which a lot of coming and going centers, although the party itself is not particularly significant. Chapter nineteen, sandwiched in between Tomoyoshi's confrontation with the deceitful Ohide at Sonoda's house and the final solution of the various mysteries surrounding everyone's parentage, is devoted almost entirely to a summation of a letter from Ninna in England. The letter, which the author says was originally written in English, was meant to soften the effect of an earlier letter, not presented to the reader, in which he praised English universities at the expense of Japan. Here he says that Japanese universities are potentially very good and if students apply themselves seriously they will be the equal of those in England within a few decades. He perceives the snobbishness inherent in the English system and is shocked at its perpetuation in that famous bastion of liberty. Ninna also warns against promoting competitive sports too vigorously, as was the fashion of the time, for he sees them as incompatible with good scholarship. He adds that he is sending his friends three books on English schools, one of which is *Tom Brown's School Days*.

This letter is reminiscent of many one still sees from Japanese abroad, so earnest and heartfelt, so concerned with making Japan a superior nation as quickly as possible. Although it is thrust into the novel at a most vexing point, keeping the reader in a quite unnecessary state of suspense, it is completely appropriate to the young men involved and confirms our impression that this must indeed be exactly what students of the time were like.

We glimpse still other aspects of the mores of the youth through these and other characters. We find Nonoguchi Seisaku who is particularly adept at extracting money from his relatives to pay for his excesses in the teahouse, and one Kiriyama Benroku whose near-sightedness leads to a ridiculous bathhouse mixup. Sugawa and Kiriyama plot to corner two of their archenemies on a dark night as they try to steal into the dormitory only to find themselves pummeling each other. All this is pure slapstick of the type most treasured by readers of Tokugawa and early Meiji fiction. It is situation comedy on a pretty mediocre level but perhaps a reasonably accurate description of the foolishness students actually engaged in.

Stylistically, *Tōsei shosei katagi* is a patchwork affair. In part it relies heavily on the Tokugawa style so close to theatrical narrative; poetic in meter and imagery, graceful, but inexact. It will be remembered that Tsubouchi had been an avid reader of Tokugawa fiction from early childhood and had developed a fondness for the theater in his student days in Nagoya and Tokyo. The influence of these two traditions, which really are one as far as language is concerned, is very strong in his early translations and in this novel. Here too we find many rhetorical passages in the Chinese style characterized by long, balanced sentences filled with weighty abstract vocabulary.

The conversations are sharp and clear. They snap along brightly and are consistent with the personalities of the various speakers. Even in this first novel, it is apparent that Tsubouchi had a genuine talent for writing conversation. It is unfortunate that the narrative is such a jumble of styles for the resulting unevenness leaves the reader with a most unpleasant over-all impression.

We know that Tsubouchi was struggling with his style. In *Shōsetsu shinzui* he speaks at length of the need for modernizing the language of fiction,[12] but both in theory and practice he was unable to reach a satisfactory solution at this date. He recommended a style that retained the simple poetic grace of Heian literature for the narrative portions, combined with dialogue appropriate to the time of the characters. Even if we were to accept his suggestion as desirable, the style of *Tōsei shosei katagi* is far from attaining this goal.

At times, Tsubouchi fails to develop his characters fully because of the retention of certain traditional stylistic devices. He frequently resorts to a time-honored technique of the Japanese theater; he has other characters tell what occurred in a scene his reader has not witnessed. Like the unfortunate practice of Western drawing-room comedy in which the maid, feather duster in hand, fills the audience in on the background of the play, it does little to bring the reader closer to the characters. Hearing details at second hand is vexing enough, but when the characters reporting the events admit they are not being accurate, the reader is thrown into confusion.

Thus, in telling the story of the incident when Yoshizumi insults Sanji and Tanoji, the narrator, a student named Tsugihara, makes frequent reference to his inability to recount the events accurately. He himself has heard about it only through some unspecified third party and does not know all the details. To strain the reader's credulity still further, Tsugihara is quite drunk and attempts to tell the story in a deliberately vague, theatrical style.

There may well be some merit in this method of exposition

[12] For a discussion of the language reform movement and Tsubouchi's efforts see my *Japan's First Modern Novel*, pp. 80–89.

that has no bearing on characterization as such. For one thing, it is the sort of stylistic tour de force in which Japanese readers take particular delight. The introduction of the language of theatrical narration into fiction would enhance its attraction for most Japanese people. They feel an intimacy born of long familiarity and consider it good artistry. The young men joke with each other, punning and parrying off one another's comments throughout the chapter, of which the Yoshizumi story is only a part. The exchange is lighthearted and good-natured. Perhaps to the Japanese the frivolous quality imposed on the incident by Tsugihara is preferable to directly witnessing the quarrel.

The effect on one's understanding of Sanji, Tanoji, and Yoshizumi is, however, unfortunate. The reader has been carefully prepared for an exciting event. On the evening of the confrontation, Sanji attends the farewell party for Ninna with Moriyama Tomosada, his friend's father. Ninna persuades Sanji, who has a severe headache, to go home. Sanji gets into a rickshaw. At the same moment, Yoshizumi and a friend are leaving that same teahouse with Tanoji and Benkichi. Sanji's driver races with the driver of the other two rickshaws and soon loses his way. They all arrive in the Yoshiwara quarter and, stumbling from the rickshaw, Sanji finds himself face to face with Tanoji and Yoshizumi.

This is the final line of chapter eight. Chapter nine is about an entirely different set of characters; it is a rambling scene linking up some of the more foolish antics of the other students. It is, for instance, in this scene that Sugawa and Kiriyama decide to corral their rivals in the dark. In the course of events Sugawa runs into one of them, Tsugihara, and as the chapter ends he is eating with his "enemy" in a restaurant. It is in chapter ten that Tsugihara gets around to telling Sugawa about the Sanji-Yoshizumi incident.

Certainly this is dramatically disappointing to the reader. Left dangling at the end of chapter eight, it would seem he deserved a greater reward for his patience than this confused account. Whatever stylistic merits the method may have, Tsubouchi has missed the opportunity to give more than a hint of Yoshizumi's vindictiveness and Tanoji's strength. In the theater there might be some justification for telling events at second hand in the interest of economy, although in this case even that would hardly seem apposite, but surely such considerations have no place in fiction. We must question whether Tsubouchi has here failed to grasp the potential of his tool.

The author also habitually does not identify the characters who appear in any given scene until they are addressed by another character. He then identifies each by name every time he speaks as one would indicate the characters in a play. Most of these delays in identification are not particularly troublesome to the reader, but there are occasions when they are most irritating. For example, chapter thirteen is, except for a short and rather lyrical descriptive opening passage, entirely devoted to the discussion between Tanoji and Sanji regarding their future relations. Although it becomes clear who is speaking after the first few exchanges, they do not call each other by name and the author labels them only as "woman" and "man" throughout the entire chapter. This is the most serious chapter in the novel and hardly the moment for games. Tsubouchi blunts the force of his material by using this jarring style.

As noted earlier, one of the most distracting qualities of *Tōsei shosei katagi* is the author's habit of interpolating personal or generalized commentary into the text at irregular intervals. Occasionally these take the form of fairly extensive moralistic essays touching on such questions as man's passions, the benighted state of Japanese women, or types of love to be encountered in this world. At one point there is a discussion of the need to dress in a manner suited to one's true position in life. It appears at the opening of chapter eighteen when the plot has reached its climax, and has virtually nothing to do with unraveling the mysteries at hand. Several pages in length, it also contains an unfortunate mistake in English. The familiar "the end justifies the means" is given as "extremities justify the means," and "extremities" is subsequently taken to mean extreme devices.

The contemporary Japanese reader would presumably not have been as diverted by this slip as we are, but Tsubouchi had a difficult time working around his error and he clearly jumbled the passage as a consequence.

The author is also at pains to defend his novel. Chapters six, seven, and ten end in comments meant to justify the introduction of what some readers criticized as vulgar language, characters, or events. Assuming the righteous tone he often used in *Shōsetsu shinzui*, Tsubouchi describes the depiction of the base and vulgar as the proper function of a novelist. "Truth" is what he seeks and "truth" encompasses the whole range of society. He also protests against the complaint that his novel lacks a political message. This, he says, would reintroduce precisely the didactic tone he had sought to eliminate.

The over-all effect of these digressions is to add a sizable quantity of words to an already complex book. They make the story even more difficult to follow and surely contribute little to its impact. Many of them are written in a dense rhetorical style that is most unpleasant to read. The style is officious and overly intellectual, having little or nothing in common with the narrative style used to describe the events taking place in the story. This is a light tale, despite its gloomier aspects, and the Victorian-Confucian quality of these intrusive passages is inimicable to the very tone of the plot. Tsubouchi had countless European models for this technique—Dickens being perhaps the most conspicuous among them—but this hardly makes it more palatable.

There was a tremendous public reaction to *Tōsei shosei katagi* when it first appeared. It was commented upon in virtually all contemporary publications, and everyone in the intellectual and artistic world seems to have read it. The most famous review is one by Tsubouchi's friend Takada Sanae that appeared in *Chūō gakujutsu zasshi* in April 1886.[13] Reacting to the criticism that the novel was coarse and vulgar, Takada establishes two cate-

[13] The review has been reprinted in the *Gendai bungakuron taikei*, vol. 1.

gories of novels; ideal novels, which, like Scott's *Waverley* and Bakin's *Hakkenden*, are romantic and unrelated to the real world; and social novels, which, like Dickens' *Pickwick Papers* and Jippensha Ikku's *Hizakurige*, reflect crosscurrents in the contemporary scene. He places *Tōsei shosei katagi* in the latter category and declares it to combine the best elements of Dickens and Thackeray. In its favor, he finds it lacking the complexities of *Pickwick Papers* and the vulgarity of *Hizakurige*, Shikitei Samba's *Ukiyoburo*, and Tamenaga Shunsui's *Shunshoku umegoyomi*.[14] Takada wonders if Tsubouchi has not been influenced by Thackeray's *Vanity Fair*, which similarly was without an identifiable hero. Komachida Sanji, a weak "hypochondriac," he feels occupies the same relative position as Becky Sharp.

On the negative side, Takada finds the main characters inadequately drawn. They are either being very eccentric, even bizarre, or they are like blocks. When European authors like Bulwer-Lytton, Dickens, and Thackeray present unusual people, they show them in normal moments as well so that they have more dimension. European writers allow their characters to reveal personality by their actions while writers of the East, including Tsubouchi, feel compelled to explain their characters in detail. Sanji is fanciful, Tomoyoshi muscular, and Sugawa mean, but none is a real person. The other characters are merely pedestrian.

Takada finds the book rich in wit and humor but lacking in pathos; it has elements of comedy but almost nothing by way of tragedy. After reading the novel through he cannot recall portions that revealed the depths of sorrow. For such pointless novels as *Hizakurige* and *Ukiyoburo*, this is a matter of little concern, but for a work that aspires to higher goals it is a serious flaw. The author fails to make adequate use of his tragic material; the love story of Sanji and Tanoji could have greatly moved his readers had Tsubouchi developed it properly.

Stylistically, Takada deplores Tsubouchi's excessive

[14] The various books mentioned by Takada are identified in my *Japan's First Modern Novel*.

dependence on puns. In both Japan and the West, he feels, such word games have been criticized as a poor means of conveying humor. While admiring the author's use of English to enhance the veracity of the students' chatter, Takada finds its presence throughout the entire text excessive to the point of being offensive.

Takada closes with a reaffirmation of his belief that *Tōsei shosei katagi* is a first-rate novel for Japan; his adverse criticism comes as a result of his comparing it with Western fiction. The author, says Takada, is but a student himself. His writing is immature and the book is too much of a diary and not enough of a novel. Now, he concludes, we await his second novel.

This was by far the most thoughtful contemporary review of the novel and it greatly impressed young intellectuals of the time.[15] It is written in a ponderous rhetorical language that would seem far more suitable for an abstract philosophical discussion than for a book review, but then literary criticism was new to Japan in those years and men were just beginning to grope for the proper language and content for the genre. Tsubouchi took this review very much to heart, probably because Takada was such a close friend, and he tried to respond to Takada's suggestions in his subsequent writing.

As we have already observed, *Tōsei shosei katagi* is often denigrated by literary historians who feel that it fails to comply with the ideals for a novel set forth in the *Shōsetsu shinzui* and is therefore unacceptable, even for its own time. The novel, however, does reflect ideas in Tsubouchi's critical writing as he and his contemporaries understood them, but not as later men have interpreted them. It must be remembered that Tsubouchi was working out of two traditions of fiction: nineteenth-century Japanese, and eighteenth- and nineteenth-century French and English. He had had no contact with Russian fiction and knew nothing of Dostoevskii's introspection, Turgenev's exquisite

[15] It was accepted as evidence of Takada's superior literary sensitivity. Ichijima Shunjō, "Meiji bungaku shoki no tsuioku," *Shōsetsu shinzui*, pp. 177–78.

brevity, or Tolstoy's expansive characterization. The European fiction he knew was rich in light-hearted adventures, humorous characters, and large groups of people moving through complex plots. Tsubouchi thought that delineation of social injustices was considered intrinsic to fiction. Coincidences and misunderstandings of the kind we find in *Tōsei shosei katagi* were hardly an invention of Tsubouchi; any Dickens novel contains a plenitude of these. What is now considered maudlin sentimentality was characteristic of Bulwer-Lytton's once esteemed novels. The romantic protestations of Tanoji are hardly less believable than those of Nina in *Rienzi*; indeed they are more acceptable today as they are more subtly expressed.

It must further be realized that twentieth-century standards for plot, structure, characterization, and emotional expression were not accepted or even understood in the nineteenth century anywhere in the world, least of all in Japan where a criticism for fiction was only just being evolved. The merits of *Tōsei shosei katagi* must be discussed in terms of the fiction that had gone before and the Western fiction Tsubouchi was trying to emulate, and not against a system of judgment codified by later men. To do so would be to create a kind of critical imperialism that implies the judgments of the twentieth century are inherently superior to those of the nineteenth, a position few contemporary intellectuals would be willing to support. Difficult though it may be, *Tōsei shosei katagi* must be seen in relation to its own time, and not as we would have liked it to have been written.

Tsubouchi clearly saw the low position of women as a major social problem. He had been visiting Sen in the Nezu quarter for a year and obviously learned a great deal about the lives of the women who lived there. Although they have virtually priced themselves out of existence today, for centuries the teahouses served an important social function in Japan much as such houses did in France. It was in the company of professional women that Japanese men relaxed in the true meaning of that word. They expressed their feelings in words in a way they could not at home because of the restraints imposed on them by the complex rules of propriety governing the Japanese family. They considered their own wives incapable of bright repartee or true wit, perhaps unjustly, and thought of professional women as the only people to whom they could talk. As we have seen, writers used these women as their material for centuries for they seemed more interesting in every way than ordinary women and because they obviously had more to say to men than did the men's own wives.

Tsubouchi viewed this situation in a different light, however, alerted as he was by his reading of English and French literature. He looked beyond the paint and the gay kimono to find what had brought the women to the quarter and held them there. The answer was obviously in the inequitable Japanese society of the time. Tsubouchi was trying to express that inequality in this plot, contrived though it is. Of course, the idea had been used by Japanese writers before, particularly in texts for Bunraku and Kabuki, but there can be no question that Tsubouchi developed the theme further than his predecessors did. He tried to do what Dickens did with a serious idea: he tried to combine humor, slapstick, and drama all in one huge novel, and while perhaps in our terms he failed, he succeeded admirably for his contemporaries.

Chapter Four

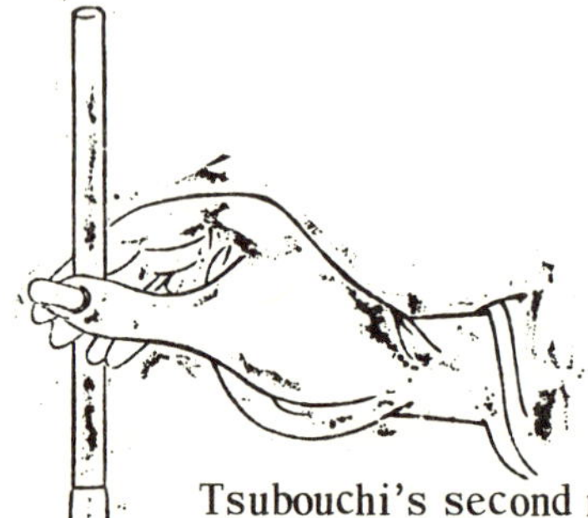

Tsubouchi's second novel, *Imotose kagami* (A Mirror of Marriage), was written between November 1885 and August 1886, encompassing the time when his future wife Sen's contract with the house in Nezu was terminated and she came to live with him. It was published in sections between January and September 1886 in the same format as his first novel. Indications are that it never had the success of *Tōsei shosei katagi* and that, despite Tsubouchi's already considerable reputation, it failed to attract widespread attention, although young intellectuals are said to have waited eagerly for each installment.[1]

One of the most interesting discoveries that can be made through careful reading of *Imotose kagami* is the great debt the fledgling writer Futabatei Shimei (1864–1909) owed to Tsubouchi. This point has been ignored in the literature but is of great importance in understanding Futabatei's development as a writer. Futabatei, still very much a student, presented himself at Tsubouchi's house in January 1886, just after his abrupt departure from the Tokyo School of Foreign Languages where he had for years been immersed in studying Russian literature. Attracted by

[1] Kawatake Shigetoshi and Yanagida Izumi, *Tsubouchi Shōyō*, pp. 152–53.

Tsubouchi's already considerable reputation as a novelist and by his essay on the novel, Futabatei obviously saw in Tsubouchi that special combination of teacher, mentor, and patron that characterizes the artistic leaders of Japan. From the time they met Tsubouchi took an active interest in Futabatei's writing and Futabatei certainly must have read *Imotose kagami* since it was the work of the man who was guiding his literary career.

After several attempts at translation in the spring of 1886, Futabatei began his first novel, *Ukigumo* (Drifting Clouds), in the summer of that year.[2] He showed drafts of the early chapters to Tsubouchi from January 1887 on. These chapters bear a strong resemblance to portions of *Imotose kagami*; Futabatei—consciously or unconsciously—borrowed considerably from Tsubouchi's novel. In some instances the similarity of style indicates that in the process of correcting Futabatei's work, Tsubouchi himself actually wrote or at least rewrote passages of his disciple's novel.

Tsubouchi's use of the term *kagami* in his title had antecedents in earlier Japanese history and literature as did the word *katagi* in the title of his first novel. *Kagami* (mirror) was originally employed in historical works to indicate an accurate account, and came to be used in the titles of plays and stories with a similar implication. Subsequently it is found in the names of handbooks of instruction of a highly didactic, moralistic nature. A "Mirror of Marriage" therefore would be a true picture of what marriage is like and would provide, by its telling, a cogent lesson for the reader. Like *katagi*, the word *kagami* in the title was meant to attract a wide audience.

The obvious parallels between events in Tsubouchi's own life and the main plot line of this story dwarfs into insignificance earlier published suggestions that the idea for the story came from an incident between two teachers of Tsubouchi's acquaintance.[3] It is in a real sense a projection of what he,

2 *Ukigumo* is translated in my *Japan's First Modern Novel*.

3 Kawatake and Yanagida, *Tsubouchi Shōyō*, p. 151. The incident involved one man's tricking another to prevent his marrying a

Tsubouchi, might do to Sen if he were to marry her. It is a kind of personalized morality play, a working out on paper of the worst possible results of an ill-conceived marriage, where the man—sensitive, intelligent, and terribly well-meaning—repeatedly makes mistakes that ultimately drive his wife to suicide.

The main character in the novel is Misawa Tatsuzō, an attractive, educated, young man born into an upper-class samurai family. The novel is essentially a study of how he came to marry Otsuji, the daughter of a fishmonger, and his treatment of her after they marry. There is also a parallel plot, the story of an ambitious young bureaucrat named Tanuma Saikitsu, who manages to win the hand of the wealthy and beautiful Oyuki. The novel becomes bogged down in the recounting of a highly complex additional subplot about Tatsuzō's father that unfortunately distracts the reader from the artistry of the author's handling of the story of Tatsuzō and Otsuji. This subplot, while essential for providing the motivation for Tatsuzō's estrangement from his bride, is certainly the least convincing part of the novel, and intrudes melodramatic kabukiesque qualities into what is otherwise a psychological novel of some depth.

The novel opens with a dream in which Tatsuzō imagines himself declaring his love for Otsuji, whom he has known for some time as a neighbor. In the dream his mother appears and admonishes him against a liaison with a woman who is his social inferior, and when he wakens, he realizes it would be best to move to new lodgings, as he has indeed become very fond of Otsuji.

We next find him at a small gathering at New Year's time. We learn that he has been frequenting the home of Nanjō Takamune, the head of the division of the bureaucracy in which he is employed. Also present is Tanuma Saikitsu, an old friend of Tatsuzō's, who has ingratiated himself with the Nanjō family and been taken into their home. The two young men in the company of the son of the Nanjō family play a traditional holiday card

---

woman they loved in common, which is indeed a facet of the plot, but hardly the crucial one.

game with the two Nanjō daughters and their friend, who turns out to be none other than Otsuji. This is the first time Tatsuzō and Otsuji have seen each other since his departure from their old neighborhood several months before; the meeting is amicable. Tatsuzō cannot avoid comparing her with Oyuki, the nineteen-year-old elder Nanjō daughter. Yes, he concludes, there is a great difference between the reticent, ill-clad Otsuji and such an elegant, refined young woman as Oyuki.

The girls retire when Takamune and his wife return, and serious drinking begins. Tatsuzō withdraws to the garden and there overhears a conversation that throws his whole life into confusion. Otsuji is speaking of Tatsuzō, praising his intelligence and appearance. Oyuki petulantly declares that she finds him bookish and arrogant, and adds that she has been hearing stories about him. She says that she would not marry him although her parents have suggested it several times. Tatsuzō retreats without listening to more.

Saikitsu and Tatsuzō leave the party together. Walking through the festive streets, they speak of the young women. Tatsuzō wonders that the Nanjō daughters are on such intimate terms with Otsuji, since they are of such a different social class, and Saikitsu explains that Otsuji's deceased mother had been their wet nurse. Furthermore Otsuji's elder sister Oharu was the concubine of a man named Kasuya, who was from the same province as Nanjō Takamune, which makes the family feel an affinity for him. Saikitsu then goes on to extol the virtues of Otsuji; her quiet, gentle disposition and her firm resolve. He points out that she has repeatedly resisted suggestions that she become a geisha and had recently turned down a young bureaucrat named Sakamoto who offered to take her as a concubine. Sakamoto, it seems, had subsequently begun courting her with the prospect of a proper marriage.

Tatsuzō is skeptical of his friend's interpretation of Otsuji's character. Knowing the family better, he is able to reconstruct some of the incidents to which his friend refers more accurately, and he realizes that Otsuji's father had been the stumbling block to negotiations over her future rather than Otsuji herself. He resists Saikitsu's hints that he should marry Otsuji, protesting that he intends to remain single as long as possible.

Saikitsu has clearly addressed himself to Tatsuzō's principal concern; he had stayed away from Otsuji because he feared what others would say if he were to marry her. Now his friend is giving his approval, indeed his encouragement, to the liaison and further offers him a piece of news that will make his decision even easier. He tells Tatsuzō that Otsuji's father is going to open a restaurant with Kasuya's help, thereby elevating the family to a far more acceptable level of the merchant class. In ruminating on Saikitsu's words after they part, Tatsuzō feels that a significant barrier to the marriage has been removed; what difference is there now between Otsuji's family and the Nanjōs?

Although obviously troubled by Otsuji's lack of education—she is in fact illiterate—he persuades himself that he can teach her since she is not stupid. Tatsuzō is attracted by her strong affection for him and feels considerable compassion for her. Jealousy is also a factor; if Sakamoto is seeking Otsuji's hand and if it is true that Oyuki is fond of Saikitsu, then he is without anyone.

He next encounters Otsuji during the cherry blossom season as she strolls along in a party composed of her father, her sister Oharu, Kasuya, and another fellow elegantly dressed in Western clothes whom Tatsuzō assumes to be Sakamoto. Tatsuzō marvels at the change in Otsuji's appearance and fears she has already married Sakamoto, with whom she is chatting intimately. Spring passes into the lonely rainy season. Tatsuzō reads a translation of Bulwer-Lytton's *Ernest Maltravers*—his first excursion into Western fiction—and is greatly impressed by the similarity between Alice and Otsuji. Ernest was able to transform the coarse, illiterate Alice into a proper English lady; why can't he do the same? Although he is only twenty-three, both of his parents are dead, and Tatsuzo is free to marry whomever he chooses, but the implications of this freedom frighten him and he is visited by the most profound doubts. By August, however, he has managed to overcome his misgivings, and he and Otsuji are married. Kasuya and Oharu serve as go-betweens.

It is not until much later in the novel that the reader's suspicions of Tanuma Saikitsu and his advice are confirmed. We learn that Saikitsu had yearned for Oyuki from the moment he first saw her and all his efforts to charm her parents stemmed from that desire. Being on the point of graduating from the same school the Nanjō's son had recently entered, he was able to befriend the boy and help him considerably with his studies. He was afraid to ask the Nanjōs for Oyuki until he was well established. Although Oyuki's mother thought Saikitsu a likely prospect, she was charmed by Tatsuzō as soon as he appeared. Watching the friendship between the elder Nanjōs and Tatsuzō flourish, Saikitsu became terrified that they would take his friend for their son-in-law before he himself had an opportunity to speak. He therefore seized upon the idea of persuading Tatsuzō to marry Otsuji as a means of disposing of a potential rival.

Less than a month after their marriage, Tatsuzō is sent to the Osaka-Kobe region to inspect oil and wax production. He is there almost three weeks when he has a chance encounter that leads him into great difficulties and that furthermore introduces the reader to the complicated subplot. Hearing cries of help on a busy Osaka street, he rushes after a thief and retrieves a bundle that was stolen from a young girl. He escorts her home and tells her his name. Next day his work is interrupted by the appearance of her mother who comes to thank him with amusing effusiveness. Soon we learn that she has another matter on her mind; the lives of her two elder daughters had been ruined by another Misawa some years before and Tatsuzō soon realizes that it was his own father, Yoshinobu, who had been the culprit.

Through her reconstruction of the past, we learn that the old woman, Kamozaki Sawae, had been born into a high-ranking samurai family, but had been married to the heir of a wealthy shop owner after refusing to accept her parents' choice of a groom.

Her husband had died while still young, leaving her with three daughters to support. The oldest girl, accomplished in the arts, had at her own insistence become a geisha, taking the name Kouno. In Osaka on official business many years before the time of the novel, Tatsuzō's father Yoshinobu had conceived a great passion for Kouno and tried to take her back to Tokyo with him. She repeatedly refused him but he stayed on and on, spending vast sums to impress her.

When it came time for Yoshinobu to return to Tokyo, it transpired that he could not pay his bill to the teahouse; indeed he could not even pay for his trip home. Kouno borrowed two hundred yen from a usurer and lent it to Yoshinobu so that he could save his reputation. Trusting him as a member of the upper classes, she had not asked him for a promissory note. Yoshinobu not only subsequently failed to return the money, he did not even answer the many pleas she had addressed to him after he returned to Tokyo.

Listless from grief, Kouno soon lost her popularity. The teahouse owner repaid fifty yen of the debt, feeling responsible in part for the girl's difficulties, but no other help was forthcoming. Kouno returned to her mother's home, by then quite ill. Threatened by the usurer, Sawae agreed to accept a short-term loan of one hundred fifty yen from a Tokyo brothel keeper. Sawae's second daughter, Oshimo, would have to serve at the brothel for two years if the debt were not repaid within the four months stipulated, but Sawae was confident that Kouno would recover her strength and begin to earn as much as she had earlier.

Unhappily, Kouno became even more seriously ill and Sawae herself, weakened by work and worry, soon took to her bed. When this new debt came due, it could not of course be repaid and Oshimo was forced to go to the brothel in Tokyo. Even before departing, she borrowed another hundred yen to have something to leave for her mother and sisters, and contracted to stay in the house for three years instead of two. Soon after Oshimo left for Tokyo her elder sister Kouno died.

Sawae began teaching in a neighborhood school and taking in

sewing, and by the time Tatsuzō meets her, she is doing relatively well. The bundle Tatsuzō had rescued from the thief contained a particularly elegant garment Sawae had made for a wealthy customer. To add to her many sorrows, Sawae has learned that Oshimo has incurred another three-hundred yen debt while in Tokyo and must continue her life as a prostitute another three years.

Tatsuzō is horrified to think that his father had been the cause of such misery. He remembers that Yoshinobu had been detained in Osaka an unexpectedly long time just before his death and realizes that this story must be true. The reader had learned earlier in the story that Yoshinobu had been a poor husband and father, leaving his wife and son alone and impoverished in their home province while he lived a comfortable life in Tokyo replete with concubine and a whole retinue of servants. He had fared well with the change of government after 1868, and had almost as substantial a position after the Restoration as before. Vain and inconstant all his life, he had originally married Tatsuzō's mother, Omiki, after casually divorcing his first wife. An orphaned relative, Omiki had been a servant in his parents' home and been made pregnant by him before their marriage. Within months he tired of Omiki as well, finding her lacking in the beauty and artistic refinements he sought in a woman.

Omiki had pressed her husband for help, begging him to come home or let her bring their son to Tokyo. After putting her off haughtily time and again, Yoshinobu had promised to see them on his way back from Osaka. This turned out to be the same trip on which he became infatuated with Kouno; he returned directly to Tokyo where he soon fell seriously ill. He lost his position and his servants left him. He had turned out his concubine even before leaving for Osaka, having heard bad reports of her behavior, and on his return discovered she had slipped back into the house in his absence and stolen many things. He was too embarrassed to even make the theft known. Yoshinobu, finally repentant, begged Omiki to bring his son to him; she arrived to find him emaciated by illness, the house neglected. It had been a separation of eight years. Soon he died of cancer, leaving an avalanche of debts.

With the help of an uncle, Yoshinobu's house and furnishings were sold. Only a small part of his total debt could be repaid however; other claims had to be ignored. Hearing of Kouno's sorrowful end these many years later, Tatsuzō realizes that amongst these debts, in a pile of unopened bills, must have been the letters urging repayment of his father's two-hundred yen loan.

Tatsuzō promises the old woman that he will repay the loan soon after the New Year. Sawae urges him instead to contact Oshimo and find out what would be needed to win her freedom. Although totally unfamiliar with the ways of the licensed quarter, Tatsuzō vows to do whatever he can to speed her release. The bond between Tatsuzō and Sawae is further strengthened when he agrees to move to her home for the balance of his stay in Osaka.

Between the trip in September and the first of the year, Tatsuzō manages to save two-hundred yen by doing translations, although it means he often has to neglect his official work. He persuades a friend to take him to the teahouse where he soon meets Oshimo, and after checking her past history determines everything is as Sawae had reported. He thereupon offers to win her release. At first she is pleased but then, to his amazement, she refuses; she has a lover and has no desire to return to Osaka. Tatsuzō is genuinely perplexed. Should he simply give her the two-hundred yen to squander on her lover, thereby fulfilling the letter of his obligation if not the intent, or should he perhaps give the money to her mother so that at least some good use would be made of it?

During these crucial weeks when he is trying to absolve his dead father's debt, Tatsuzō fails to tell his wife anything about the problem. Almost by default, he has neglected to keep her abreast of his activities, and she has grown ever more suspicious and insecure. Otsuji is painfully aware of her inadequacies; when she sees that he is spending his evenings away and saving money for unspecified reasons, she immediately concludes he is interested in other women. Tatsuzō for his part had become aware of the difficulties inherent in his marriage early enough. Even while in Osaka, he had been struck by his own reticence to write an affectionate letter to his bride, knowing it must be read to her by someone else. After his return to Tokyo, he had become completely absorbed in translating for the money he needed to repay the debt, and he and Otsuji had become more and more estranged. Although she struggles to learn to read and write, her progress is inadequate to her ambitions and she is constantly aware of her dependence on others to read the simplest things.

The morning after Oshimo has rejected Tatsuzō's offer, a letter arrives at their home in his absence. Otsuji finds it and, after some debate, opens it. She is able to make out little enough of what it says but she realizes it is from a woman of the quarter. When Tatsuzō returns and finds she has opened the letter, he is angry; soon he relents however for he knows his protracted silence is to blame. Thereupon he tells her the whole story, in a cold and objective fashion, and even reads her the letter, which turns out to be an apology from Oshimo. For no particular reason, he fails to read the postscript to the letter. At first Otsuji is quite suspicious of his explanation but eventually she comes to accept it.

Next day Tatsuzō leaves, announcing he will stop that afternoon at the home of his sponsor, a man named Kimura, and then call on Oshimo as she had requested in the letter. In his absence, Otsuji's elder sister Oharu comes to call and in the course of her visit completely shatters the peace of mind Otsuji had so dearly won. Knowing that Tatsuzō earns some eighty yen a month and has outside income as well, Oharu has come to try to secure regular support for their father from her sister's husband.

Oharu has had a checkered career, most recently having been turned out by Kasuya, and is just now recovering from a serious illness probably induced by her dissipation. The restaurant their father Kyūhachi had opened with Kasuya's help had fallen into disrepute, largely because of the old man's belligerent behavior when drinking and because of the notoriety of Oharu's affairs.

Kyūhachi has decided to close the restaurant and return to peddling fish. Otsuji is faintly repelled by her sister's drinking and deportment, but is obviously in awe of her sophistication. As they talk we learn that Oharu's dissipation is of long standing indeed. It transpires that it was she who had been the concubine of Tatsuzō's father those many years before, who had stolen so much from him, and been turned out shortly before his death. It is only when she presses Otsuji for money that the story Tatsuzō had told his wife the evening before comes out and Oharu realizes whose son he is.

In attempting to persuade Otsuji to give their father money, Oharu moves from flattery to abuse in successive stages. She is a clever woman; she knows exactly how to weaken Otsuji's defenses. By the time she is through, Otsuji is wracked by fear and doubt. In some part at least, the author assures us, this is because Oharu cannot really believe Tatsuzō's story. Being of such base instincts herself, she is certain that no prostitute would refuse an offer of money and no man would make it except in the expectation of the woman's coming to live with him. When she reads Oshimo's letter of apology, which Otsuji rescues from the garbage, she interprets it as a response to a lover's quarrel. She naturally makes much of Tatsuzō's neglect to read the postscript. It actually is yet another apology in the same tone as the body of the letter but, because of the ambiguities of language, can be interpreted as meaning that Oshimo is holding out for what she wanted in a quarrel with Tatsuzō. Oharu concludes that he has offered to make her his concubine and that Oshimo will settle for nothing less than becoming his wife.

Realizing that Tatsuzō will not return home that night, Oharu stays with Otsuji and the two sisters agonize over schemes that might save the marriage. Tatsuzō's failure to return is interpreted as further evidence of his guilt. They decide that Otsuji should seek advice from Kimura, Tatsuzō's old benefactor, and that Oharu should try to persuade Oshimo to give Tatsuzō up.

Meanwhile, Tatsuzō has been having a most disturbing evening. In speaking with Kimura, he discovers that the older man has been informed of Tatsuzō's visits to the quarter. Although Kimura has been unhappy about his marriage from the first, he admonishes Tatsuzō for his lack of caution, and lectures him on the tendency of wives to gossip. Kimura seems to imply that Otsuji has been telling someone about his trips to the quarter, and Tatsuzō precipitously and incorrectly concludes she had been to see Kimura. Tatsuzō is furious at this evidence of disloyalty and thinks he may well divorce Otsuji. But he decides she meant no harm, and it would be intellectually dishonest to send her away on such a pretext. She is again acting just as one would expect an ignorant person to act.

Upon leaving Kimura's house, Tatsuzō stops to eat in a cheap eel shop. There he overhears servants gossiping. After some moments it becomes apparent that they are speaking of the marriage of Tanuma Saikitsu and Oyuki, which is apparently a farce. Saikitsu, they say, fawns upon his wife in a most unseemly fashion while his mother complains endlessly that she is being neglected. Saikitsu's mother is a provincial woman with no experience in handling a household and is the laughingstock of the servants. The servants have overheard Oyuki trying to instruct her husband in ways to soothe his mother's pride.

As he listens in amusement, it comes to Tatsuzō for the first time that his friend had deliberately persuaded him to marry Otsuji so that he would be out of the way. He suspects that Saikitsu had also turned Oyuki against him. Even more dispirited than before, he decides to go home rather than trying once more to persuade Oshimo to leave the brothel. He lets himself into the house and overhears his wife and sister-in-law talking at exactly the moment Oharu realizes that Tatsuzō is Yoshinobu's son. Sickened by the thought that Otsuji is the sister of such a woman, he retreats without announcing himself.

It has been a night of unhappy revelations for Tatsuzō. Unable to think of a place to go, he turns to Kasuya, in part because Kasuya is known to stay up late and in part because, if there is to be a divorce, Kasuya having been the go-between ought to be informed. There is much drinking and chatter, but when Kasuya and Tatsuzō finally lie down to sleep, Tatsuzō tells him of his difficulties with Otsuji. Kasuya offers no serious objection to a divorce; like Kimura, he had seen how poor a match it was from the beginning. He suggests that he thought Tatsuzō had acted overromantically in marrying Otsuji at all.

In the morning, Tatsuzō returns home, breakfasts, changes his clothes, and leaves for work without exchanging more than half a dozen words with Otsuji. Nearly frantic, she rushes to see Kimura. He accepts her version of Tatsuzō's affair with Oshimo as confirmation of the rumors he had heard earlier. In an attempt to reassure Otsuji, Kimura promises to speak sternly to Tatsuzō at once.

The next day Otsuji's world is thrown into complete turmoil. Tatsuzō is at work when the maid announces the arrival of Kamozaki Sawae and her youngest daughter. At that very moment, Tatsuzō comes storming in, a newspaper clutched in his hand, and he and the visitors closet themselves in a reception room without even speaking to Otsuji.

Unable to contain herself, she listens at the door. Tatsuzō, in open fury, tells Sawae that he will divorce his wife because of the disgrace she has brought upon him. An article has appeared in the paper reporting that his wife had gone to the teahouse and asked Oshimo to stop seeing him. The article elaborates on his repeated visits to the quarter, his neglect of his official duties, and his affection for Oshimo. It suggests furthermore that he will be dismissed from his post as a consequence. Sawae is sickened by the realization that she is responsible for all this and vainly tries to calm him. They leave the house soon after.

Otsuji rushes into the empty room and tries to read the article. She can make out only the word "dismissed" and is close to hysteria when Oharu arrives. Her sister is flushed with triumph; it was she who had been to see Oshimo and she has learned that Tatsuzō's version of the events is true and that the prostitute wants nothing to do with him. Thus she feels she is the bearer of most happy news and is astounded to find Otsuji capable only of weeping and mumbling incoherently. Oharu had come expecting her sister to reward her for her efforts and certain that assurance of the continuation of her marriage would prompt Otsuji to promise her father and sister a future income, but instead she is greeted by tears. Infuriated, Oharu reverts to her coarsest nature and lashes out at Otsuji, attacking her ingratitude. She storms out of the house warning Otsuji never to come near her or their father again.

Just as Oharu exits in a fury, Tatsuzō returns. He coldly announces to his wife that he is sending her home to her father and will listen to no further excuses or explanations from her. He leaves the house abruptly. To whom can Otsuji turn now? She thinks again of Kimura and tries to find some glimmer of hope.

The article in the newspaper actually came about because a reporter had been in a room in the teahouse adjoining the one in which Oharu had spoken to Oshimo. Listening from somewhere in the middle of their conversation, he had tried to piece the story together, and then talked it over with others in the teahouse who knew Oshimo to fill in certain details. The article as it appeared had just enough veracity to be convincing and Tatsuzō no doubt is correct in assuming it will never be forgotten.

In the last chapter of the novel, we find Oyuki and a former servant alighting from a rickshaw and walking up an embankment. Whenever she comes to this spot, the maid says quietly, she is reminded of Otsuji and how she drowned herself here. The maid tries to say that she feels Tatsuzō was to blame; Oyuki interrupts her, suggesting that it is not their place to assign blame. Oyuki adds that she envies Otsuji. Startled, the maid asks if anything is wrong with Oyuki's marriage. The young woman fails to give any explanation, merely reiterating that she wishes she had not been so well educated. She hints that her education keeps her from committing suicide. No one in Japan can understand her dilemma. With her words, "I am a wretched person," the novel ends.

Tsubouchi seems to have lost control of the story of Saikitsu and Oyuki, perhaps because he became too interested in Tatsuzō's mistake. It is apparent from the early chapters that he intended something in the way of a parallel set of marriages, but somehow Tsubouchi fails to develop the idea and we are left with a disturbingly incomplete story.

Chapter eleven, which is just halfway through the novel, is devoted to a recapitulation of events in the lives of Saikitsu and Oyuki before their marriage. Oyuki has just been informed by her mother of Saikitsu's proposal and she is by no means completely overjoyed at the prospect of marrying him. She has seen through his sycophancy and although she realizes he behaved as he did in the hope of winning her, she is offended by his manner. She is aware too that his rapid success in the bureaucracy—he is already earning eighty yen a month—is due to manipulating people. In all, she does not find him admirable. She had however previously refused another offer and is afraid her parents will stop asking her opinion and marry her to someone totally unsuited. Here we learn that Oyuki has been keeping a fan Tatsuzō had left at New Year's time; her maid takes this as evidence of her fondness for the young man. Oyuki reflects with regret on how Tatsuzō so quickly vanished from their lives and wonders if Otsuji told him what she said that night they played cards. She had, it seems, spoken as she did only to keep people from gossiping about her being fond of Tatsuzō. Oyuki of course had no way of knowing that Tatsuzō had overheard her and how her words affected his life.

Unfortunately that fateful conversation had been overheard by her mother as well as Tatsuzō, and her mother had taken it as evidence that Oyuki liked Saikitsu and disliked Tatsuzō. When Saikitsu's offer came in the fall, there was no good reason to refuse him and they were married. This is all we learn of their marriage except for the conversation Tatsuzō overhears in the eel shop. The servants who are gossiping are being very arch indeed and it is difficult to know how seriously one is supposed to take their story. The image of Saikitsu fawning on Oyuki somehow does not ring true and one wishes for direct exchanges between husband and wife rather than this flippant interpretation by the servants.

What then are we to make of this last chapter? Oyuki is obviously unhappy—her former servant notices that she is thin and pale—and has thought of suicide herself. Although its chief function is to bring the reader news of Otsuji's death, the chapter is also intended to reveal something about Oyuki. What does she mean by saying that no one in Japan can understand her? Is she implying that she is overeducated—she is a normal school graduate—for the role of a Japanese housewife? Her mother-in-law is apparently dreadful and she is not in love with her husband. Her education may well make her situation even more difficult to bear. Her life then is no more happy than Tatsuzō's.

* * * * * * *

The marriage of Otsuji and Tatsuzō had been doomed from the start. Everywhere he turns, Tatsuzō finds someone to tell him it was a mistake. Even in encouraging the match, Saikitsu casually suggests that Tatsuzō can easily divorce Otsuji if the marriage does not work out. Although Tatsuzō is shocked at his friend's callousness and reflects on the weakness of an institution that permits such ready escape, he quickly accepts this solution when things become uncomfortable for him.

Of course he has largely created the discomfort himself by his seemingly unnecessary silence. In trying to compensate the Kamozaki family for his father's misdeed, he is acting out of pure motives; why then not tell Otsuji the whole story? Does he feel she is too ignorant to understand? Is he ashamed to let her know what sort of man his father was? Unfortunately, although the author expounds at great length on the need for openness in marriage, he does not investigate this point, and the reader is left to conjecture for himself.

In any case it is apparent that once they are living together Tatsuzō is repelled by Otsuji's ignorance and is not at all up to playing Ernest Maltravers. The reader sees Otsuji only briefly through an outsider's eyes but it is a revealing glimpse. In an exchange with their maid, she shows herself to be totally inadequate in running a household. Her economies are pathetic and her attempts to direct matters hopelessly confused. Tatsuzō treats her as a *rusuban*, a person left to guard the house, and barely speaks to her as he goes about his business. He is aware that he has failed to carry out his plans to educate her and is therefore at fault, but he is not willing or able to devote time to the project. He is sometimes inadvertently cruel to her as when he reads Otsuji the letter of apology from Oshimo and comments on the hopelessness of members of the lower classes without considering how he may be hurting her.

At one point, the author suggests that Tatsuzō's great mistake was in believing he could educate his wife at all. Japanese people mature far earlier than Westerners, Tsubouchi asserts, rather naïvely, and by the time they married Otsuji's personality was determined for life. We can accept this at least as proof that the author saw the project as hopeless from the start. Tsubouchi has not given us any real evidence that she cannot be educated since no one really does anything to help her.

Despite his brutal coldness, we cannot help but pity Tatsuzō. It is true as he himself comments toward the end of the novel that he was ruined not because he had done something disgraceful but because he had tried to do something ordinarily considered commendable. He is misunderstood by everyone, even apparently by the prostitute Oshimo who does not seem able to determine what he wants of her. People like Kimura, to whom he is under great obligation—Kimura had lent him the money for his education and Tatsuzō is in the process of paying it back—immediately suspect him of the worst and are quick to believe any evidence that appears to support the rumors they have heard. Tatsuzō is highly placed in the bureaucracy for so young a man, and he will surely be let go now that it has been publicly stated that he has been neglecting his duties for frivolous reasons.

What is so distressing about him is the alacrity with which he blames Otsuji for his troubles. He seems to lash out at her at the least opportunity although he knows full well that he is far more to blame than she. Part of this at least is a display of the familiar Japanese male attitude of superiority, but part too is a reflection of his annoyance at the stupidity of his choice of a bride. It had never occurred to him that Otsuji might be so desperate as to kill herself and we can only imagine how great his despair was when he discovered what he had done. He is not stupid or insensitive, but he has been responsible for the death of a girl barely eighteen years old, with whose care he had been entrusted.

There is of course an implicit contrasting of the generations between the Misawas, father and son. During the long night as Oharu and Otsuji struggle to understand what is happening to Otsuji's marriage, Oharu suggests that while he seems a virtuous enough person on the surface, Tatsuzō cannot be trusted because he is Yoshinobu's son. In many respects Tatsuzō is maintaining the strictest virtue in what appears to be a direct reaction to his father's immorality. Unlike many of his fellow students, he had never been to a teahouse or had an affair. The respectable Oyuki describes him as stuffy and the prostitute Oshimo thinks him a bore. When confronted with Sawae's pathetic story, he immediately pledges to repay the debt and all his subsequent actions are based on a desire to salvage what he can of his father's reputation. He even fails to tell his sponsor Kimura why he is visiting the quarter in the hope of not having to reveal his father's misdeeds.

In one significant respect, however, father and son are similar; both married women their social and intellectual inferiors. There is a profound irony in Tatsuzō's lack of reflection on the misery his mother Omiki experienced at his father's hands, and in never realizing that he is doing the same thing to Otsuji although he is acting from an entirely different set of motives. Tatsuzō's mother was aware of her inadequacy just as Otsuji is a generation later, but neither woman is able to convince her husband of her essential worth. Omiki, of course, lived long enough to be reconciled finally with her husband, having at least the consolation of being needed in his final illness when all others had deserted him.

Otsuji has no function after her marriage; she is living in an essentially hostile environment. By marrying so far above her class she has isolated herself from her natural companions and has no one but her husband from whom to seek understanding. In less than two months after their marriage, Tatsuzō embarks on a project that devours his time, and she is thrust completely from his life. For some four months Otsuji can only hover helplessly in the background as Tatsuzō busies himself earning the money he feels will symbolically erase his father's sin. Here the author has done a remarkable piece of characterization for she is an essentially inarticulate woman, having no language to express her fears and resentment. Her slovenliness after marriage, her total inability to cope, her grating ignorance are all expressed both with great force and compression. Often only a line or two describing how she stood or walked will be profoundly revealing of her nature. Although she cannot express herself in words to the reader, she has our complete sympathy; there is no question that the author sees her as the victim of the selfish decision of a foolish young man.

Oharu is by far the best drawn minor character. She is magnificent as she bends her opponents to her will, flying into towering rages, soothing with soft words. She makes capital of every favor she has done for anyone and is as calculating with her father as she is with Otsuji. Her failure to listen to Otsuji's explanations in their final encounter is perhaps overdone but even that is not entirely inconsistent with her egotistical personality.

* * * * * * *

Imotose kagami is a very different novel from *Tōsei shosei katagi* both in design and effect. In a sense it is more ambitious, since it tries to probe human motivation on a more subtle level. Gone for the most part are the digressions into boyish humor and gone too are at least some of the subplots. The silly gossiping servants, the heavy dependence on coincidence, and the overly detailed history of the Kamozaki family are relics of the earlier concept of the novel, but here we have something entirely new as well. Tsubouchi has lavished space on his characters in a way unimagined in his first book. While reading *Imotose kagami* we realize that the author has discovered at last one of the great secrets of Western fiction; the need to take time, to be expansive, to let characters speak for themselves on different occasions and to different people. He uses interior monologues, he permits the minds of his characters to roam at will—in short, he employs many of the tools of modern novelists the world over.

This is not to imply that all of *Imotose kagami* is well written, for it is not. The book is stuffed with digressions by the author on everything from filial piety to the dangers of eavesdropping. Borrowing from earlier "mirror" books, the author uses the plot as a springboard for lectures on morality, largely, but not exclusively, as it has to do with marriage. Such heavy-handed moralizing does not fit in with a modern psychological novel and results in a general unevenness. Most of the moralistic discourses are poorly expressed; mixed metaphors abound and the reasoning is imperfect in the extreme.

Although he has happily abandoned the heavy obscure language he used for didactic passages in *Tōsei shosei katagi*, Tsubouchi has not really developed a style over which he has complete control. He does attempt to unify his style, however, by continuing the flowing classical literary style from one part of the novel to the other, making no distinction between descriptions of action and moralistic digressions. Except for the dialogue, which once more is brilliantly handled, this style has little in common with the spoken language. It has a soft and gracious rhythm and, although it is greatly given to ambiguity, would clearly be more intelligible to a nonintellectual audience than the language of his first novel. One senses a restraint too in the use of English and allusions to English literature, perhaps in response to criticism of the earlier book. Tsubouchi identifies his characters clearly each time they speak, and one experiences much less difficulty in following the plot than in his earlier work. This book is considered important in Japan because of the way the dialogue was printed; it is the first time the words of different speakers were written on separate lines, an innovation that helped considerably in the clarification of a text.[4]

In this second novel Tsubouchi shows himself to be the master of the incisive scene. Most often these are of short duration. There are however a few that sustain themselves over several pages; the scene in which Oharu approaches Otsuji for money for their father is the most striking example. Unfortunately Tsubouchi still seems possessed by an obsession to break into his best scenes with diversions of various sorts; sometimes with interludes concerning other characters entirely, sometimes with moralistic digressions. Both kinds of distraction have the effect of destroying any cumulative dramatic tension, and again the same disappointment is felt as when the narrative line was broken in *Tōsei shosei katagi*. It is now handled more skillfully however. Tsubouchi is approaching the Dickensian technique of suspended animation, but he has not yet achieved it.

Tsubouchi, or at least the voice of the author, is so much a part of *Imotose kagami*, speaking out as he does time and again, that we cannot help but examine his own position on the matters he discusses. Most conspicuous are his feelings about love and marriage. He describes marriage as the very cornerstone of society, an institution to be viewed with reverence. He does not argue either for or against arranged marriages, but he clearly does not feel that choosing one's own spouse is any guarantee of success. Nor can he be said to be attributing infallibility to the traditional Japanese method, for the dangers inherent in that system are apparent enough in the story of Saikitsu and Otsuji. Tsubouchi asks that men use reason, rather than passion, in choosing a bride. Think of what she will be in later life, he insists, not what she looks like now. What kind of mother will she be for your children, what kind of companion will she make for your declining years? The story itself demonstrates that one cannot expect to transform one's bride; she must be properly educated from the start.

[4] Kawatake and Yanagida, *Tsubouchi Shōyō*, p. 153.

A marriage, says Tsubouchi, is built on mutual trust and respect and without these feelings nothing but disaster will result. He chides Tatsuzō over and over for his secretiveness, his disrespect of Otsuji, and his scorn of her ignorance. The author predicts an unhappy end to the marriage from the time it is conceived—although he by no means prepares us for the extent of the tragedy—and announces that Tatsuzō has totally confused emotion with love.

Tsubouchi also chastens his hero for disregarding the advice of his mother not to marry beneath his station, although of course the advice was given in a dream. Not only was this demonstrably unfortunate; the mere fact that he failed to obey her wishes after her death is seen as morally reprehensible. In the course of the novel, Tsubouchi appears to relent in his strict interpretation of traditional filial behavior, and we are later given a surprisingly modern analysis of the conflict between the generations. The author indicates that he sees the differences in the education of parents raised in the Tokugawa tradition and children of the Meiji period cannot be easily reconciled, but expresses a hope for an early end to the open conflicts occurring in his time.

Even when the author ceases to speak in his own voice, we find comments that indicate what seemed to him to be the important issues of his time. For example, his characters discuss courtship and marriage practices in France and England. They compare them with those in Japan and find the Japanese closer to the French system in which the young man asked a girl's parents permission to begin a courtship. They feel it would require a major social upheaval for the English system of open courtship to be accepted in Japan. They go on to wonder if the prevalence of extramarital affairs in both France and Japan is not because the young people do not know each other well before they marry.

The depth of the author's concern for the plight of Japanese women is apparent throughout *Imotose kagami*. The victimization of females in Japan had been at issue in *Tōsei shosei katagi* but here the theme is developed to a far greater degree. The entire plot is, of course, built around this idea, but the subtlety with which it is expressed reveals the extent of the author's feeling. He generally does not intrude on the narrative with essays on this subject; he lets the action and the characters carry the burden of the proof, and they do it effectively. The reader nearly grows to hate Tatsuzō simply from the way he struts in and out of the house; his father's parallel cruelty to his mother touches one even though we learn of it only in a rapidly stated flashback sequence. This is superior handling of a theme and marks a significant advance in Tsubouchi's novelistic technique.

We will never know what was in Tsubouchi's mind as he wrote this novel. The analogy with his own situation is so obvious, however, that it can hardly be ignored. Like Tatsuzō, Tsubouchi had lost his parents by 1885 and was free to make his own mistakes. Was he perhaps expressing his doubts about his ability to maintain a successful marital relationship with Sen, did he fear that he too might be acting out of selfish motives and might similarly destroy her? Was he saying that he might not be up to the task of educating her? Or was this his way of airing all the arguments others had offered against the marriage thereby hoping to relegate them to oblivion? By comparison with Tatsuzō, Tsubouchi was a sophisticated man; perhaps he felt that he could carry off the marriage easily; reeducating his wife with no one any the worse for the experience, but somehow one doubts his confidence in the face of this story.

Of some things we can be sure. Tsubouchi was certainly concerned about the dire consequences of an ill-conceived marriage and had grave misgivings about men marrying beneath their social class. He was also emotionally drawn to lower-class women and scornful of the men who misused them. The parallel Saikitsu and Oyuki marriage suffers from a superficiality in treatment; the author does not know Oyuki as well as he knows Otsuji and her family. Tokyo shopkeepers, restaurant and teahouse people, geisha and prostitutes were a real part of Tsubouchi's entire adult life. He understood their pettiness, their ignorance, and their greed in a way that bespeaks long and close observation. Most of all, he recognized the reality of their suffering. For Saikitsu we feel amusement and some scorn; for Oyuki a passing regret. But Tsubouchi really cares about what happens to Otsuji and this is precisely what makes the story effective.

The Kamozaki subplot takes on added significance when we realize Tsubouchi was considering marrying Sen while writing the novel. Tatsuzō is utterly revolted when he learns that Oshimo was forced into prostitution because of his father. Through Tatsuzō, the author expresses a loathing for the bestiality of prostitution that is almost without precedent in Japanese literature. This statement alone might be accepted as the reaction of a man made sensitive to the failings of his own people by education in a foreign literature, for certainly Tsubouchi had been frequently exposed to such ideas in European novels. Since we know of the author's familiarity with the quarter, however, it reveals the true depths of his rage against the system and tells us that he was emotionally prepared to act in whatever way necessary to rescue a woman from that life.

The novel is permeated with a sense of class consciousness. The main plot and its parallel marriage, and the subplot as well, hinge around matters of social rank. Taken together with the material in Tsubouchi's first novel, we appear to have ample evidence to conclude that Tsubouchi himself accepted without too much question most of the social conventions of his day. He does not really seem to be arguing against the realities of Meiji life; he accepts the structure of society without radical suggestions for change. We do not find him objecting to the belief that there are distinctions between social classes, and that human behavior is contingent upon one's birth. All of his characters indicate his own acceptance of the belief that "birth will tell." This is apparent in everything from the resolve of Tanoji in *Tōsei shosei katagi* to the utter defeat of Otsuji in this second novel, and even in the behavior of such minor characters as Kamozaki Sawae, whose high rank at birth is carefully noted, and no doubt is meant to account for her fortitude. The dangers inherent in marrying out of one's social class is, of course, a major theme of this novel and appears completely verified by the plot.

The specific focus of Tsubouchi's attack on society is, of course, its treatment of women. He is talking about the dehumanization inherent in both prostitution and the marital system. While he makes no connection between the aristocratic society of his time and the position of women within it, he does present a clear, cogent argument for reform in the role of women in Japan. He seems to have no ready solutions, but he wants change and he is using fiction as a means of exposing an evil in much the same way as Dickens.

There is a strong possibility that this thinking was too advanced for his time, that the popular failure of this novel was due to its being concerned with issues his contemporaries were not ready to take in hand. While there was a lot of talk about the role of women in the 1880s, perhaps most readers were not inclined to undertake a serious study of the problem. The didactic digressions, overuse of coincidence, and complicated subplot would never bother his Meiji readers for they were all too accustomed to such elements and probably enjoyed them. They might, however, be troubled by a novel where a young man of the most respected class is shown as behaving badly to his wife, much though she had presumed by marrying above her proper rank. There is also some possibility that they were not interested in a psychological novel of the kind Tsubouchi was trying to put together here.

In analyzing the connection between this novel and Futabatei's famous *Ukigumo* we should direct our attention to specific scenes and to certain of the characters. Two scenes stand out: Oyuki as she watches the evening settling on the city, hearing the sounds of night, and thinking of marrying Saikitsu finds an almost direct counterpart in the first pages of the fourth chapter of *Ukigumo*; a picture of Tatsuzō's mother swirls into an image of Otsuji in the way that *Ukigumo*'s hero Bunzō confuses his mother's picture with his adored Osei and then her spiteful mother Omasa. More subtle is the similarity between the scene in which Oharu breaks down Otsuji's defenses and the one in which Omasa devastates Bunzō. And again, Tatsuzō often argues and reasons with himself in terms strongly resembling those used by Bunzō. Saikitsu, the manipulator of people, is not unlike Honda Noboru, long considered the epitome of the successful Meiji bureaucrat.

There can be little doubt therefore that *Imotose kagami* had great influence on Futabatei while he was writing *Ukigumo*. Furthermore it seems extremely likely that Tsubouchi himself wrote several pages of the manuscript of *Ukigumo* for nothing else would easily explain the similarities in style. While we may never know precisely how much of Futabatei's novel Tsubouchi contributed, his role was clearly a major one. Interestingly enough, although Tsubouchi's part in the writing of *Ukigumo* was eventually forgotten, many of the novel's original readers were completely aware of it for *Ukigumo* was first published with Tsubouchi's name given as the author. The novel was published in three parts over as many years; part one lists him as the sole author, while he is given as the coauthor of part two. Only the third and final portion of the novel was published under Futabatei's own name. Since it was a fairly common practice of the period for established authors to lend their names to books by unknown writers, literary historians have accepted this as the reason Tsubouchi's name was used. Given the evidence at hand, it now seems likely that Tsubouchi actually had enough to do with the creation of *Ukigumo* to warrant the use of his name.

Much has been said about the accuracy of Futabatei's portrayal of women and critics have groped about attempting, in vain, to find the model for the vivacious, lively Osei, heroine of *Ukigumo*. It must be remembered that we are dealing with a society where ordinarily men simply do not know women as men do in the West. Unlike Tsubouchi, Futabatei did not frequent the licensed quarter as a student and seems to have had no experience with women as a youth. Where then, critics have been asking for years, did Futabatei learn so much about women? Surely some of his understanding came from reading Tsubouchi's novels, from observing Tsubouchi's own life, and from Tsubouchi's specific assistance in writing *Ukigumo*. Futabatei was an apt pupil; Osei and her waspish mother Omasa are vibrant, dynamic characters of complex dimension. Tsubouchi may only have set the tone for the characters and suggested aspects of the plot, but the significance of his influence must be recognized.

Even more startling is the failure of critical literature to discern any connection between developments in Futabatei's personal life, *Imotose kagami*, and Tsubouchi's marriage. Futabatei's biographers are well aware of his own marriage to a prostitute, legally consummated in 1893, but none has mentioned the intellectual and emotional climate established by Tsubouchi's example, which made such a decision on Futabatei's part at least conceivable. Futabatei's marriage, like Tatsuzō's in the novel, was to end in failure, in part, at least, for the same reason, Futabatei and his wife, Tsune, were also unable to bridge the great gap in basic intellect and education existing between them. In Futabatei's case other factors militated against the endurance of the marriage; Futabatei's parents were still alive and they were vociferous in their objections to his marriage. Futabatei and Tsune were inept at managing their finances and consequently unable to be independent of his parents. Ultimately Futabatei was forced to divorce Tsune, with whom he had had two children. She was found to be pregnant with another man's child and Futabatei, who had been resisting continuous pressure from his parents to divorce his wife, was no longer able to defend her against their attacks.[5]

Thus Futabatei's marriage, almost certainly suggested by Tsubouchi's, can be viewed as yet another acting out of the scenario presented in *Imotose kagami*. Pathetic though it may seem in retrospect, Futabatei must have followed Tsubouchi in believing in the validity of such a gesture; he must have seen

[5] In his biography, *Futabatei Shimei den*, Nakamura Mitsuo reviews the few available primary sources on Futabatei's marriage and suggests various interpretations of the material. He does not, of course, see any connection with Tsubouchi's life and work (pp. 175–217).

some intrinsic value in marrying a woman whose background and experience were so different from his own. Amazingly enough, neither he nor Tsubouchi heeded the message of the novel itself; each seemed to feel he would be better able to work out his marriage than Tatsuzō. Tsubouchi and Sen managed to keep their marriage alive for nearly half a century; Futabatei's efforts brought him despair.

Tsubouchi in turn appears to have learned much about the craft of fiction from Futabatei. After Futabatei's death in 1909, Tsubouchi often referred to his debt to the younger man, although he is not specific about the nature of that debt. Futabatei seems to have been able to expand Tsubouchi's knowledge of fictional technique beyond the confines of the British experience through his understanding of the great works of Russian literature. Of major significance to Tsubouchi's own development as a novelist was the notion that working within a confined area would allow for greater depth of characterization. For example, the next novel we study, *Matsu no uchi*, is basically the story of one man and encompasses only the briefest space of time; it is in marked contrast to the sweeping canvas Tsubouchi had worked on earlier. Such a concept characterized much of the Russian fiction Futabatei admired and was the basis for the construction of his *Ukigumo*. It seems likely that this point was discussed by the two men and that its validity became apparent to both men virtually simultaneously as they worked on their own fiction.

The relationship between the two writers must have been very complex; they were both high-strung individuals struggling against almost overwhelming odds to create a modern Japanese idiom in fiction. It is obvious from *Imotose kagami* how difficult it was for Tsubouchi to abandon the Japanese literary traditions on which he had been weaned and to properly assess the Western fiction he read. The mere fact that he felt compelled to tell the unlikely story of Oshimo and her mother and sisters in such detail is ample evidence of his problems. He must have felt that such melodrama is the stuff of which fiction is made and that there could be no novel without it, when of course he had the material for a fine book with the story of Tatsuzō and Otsuji alone. Then having forced the tale of Yoshinobu's misdeeds on his readers, he fails to draw the analogy between the Misawa father and son with the clarity it deserves. It should have been an important theme in the book and not relegated to a passing suggestion, for it would have given the novel the dimension peculiar to a tale of many generations. One suspects Tsubouchi had such an idea in mind—for why else would he say so much about the elder Misawa—but here as elsewhere in the novel, the author has failed to do all he could with his materials.

In *Imotose kagami* Tsubouchi has again introduced the techniques of the theater into his novel. The most obvious—and in some ways most painful—example is the last chapter in which Otsuji's suicide is told through a conversation between the lovely, wealthy Oyuki and her former maid. As in the theatrical interludes in *Tōsei shosei katagi*, we are not satisfied novelistically by this device. The shock of the news of Otsuji's death is so great that the reader is at first uncritical of the author's presentation, but on reflection realizes that this is poor writing indeed. The novel form allows us direct experience; we do not have to hear of events at second hand as we do in the theater. One cannot help but wonder why Tsubouchi was so reluctant to express emotion directly, particularly at such a crucial moment.

Here perhaps we see most clearly how difficult it was for Tsubouchi and his contemporaries to find a voice for the new literature. We begin to suspect that Tsubouchi is actually avoiding the most significant moments in the lives of his characters because of an inability to express them satisfactorily. Since, as we have seen, Japanese is a language of inarticulation, of suggestion rather than statement, Tsubouchi may simply not have been able to come up with the words to describe the desperation of a woman as she commits suicide, as he may have been unable to create the scene in which Tanoji defends her lover in his first novel. Perhaps here too he felt some resistance to presenting a highly emotional moment at first hand, preferring the use of suggestion to the actuality. We will discover that even in his last novel, which is in so many ways a successful piece of fiction, he is unable to relate a crucial scene directly and resorts once again to a recounting of events after the fact.

There is a particular form of punctiliousness common to Japanese intellectuals that is characterized by a heightened sensitivity to disarray and a subsequent avoidance of direct confrontation and of moments requiring prompt decisions. Japanese writers of the twentieth century often choose to avoid plot altogether rather than cope with intense interplay between characters and dramatic conclusions. In his fiction, Tsubouchi appears to be caught between two forces; one his natural inclination to avoid confrontation and challenge, and the other his recognition of how essential dramatic scenes were to the European novels he was reading. His masterful scenes such as the one in *Imotose kagami* where the powerful Oharu batters her young sister's belief in Tatsuzō, are almost without equal in later Japanese fiction, for Tsubouchi knew more about creating emotionally charged situations in a novel than most of his successors. Still, he too hesitated, and seemed either too afraid or perhaps too weary to write such scenes consistently throughout a work. Eventually such emotionalism proved inimical to the Japanese literary nature, and the greatest writers of the twentieth century have chosen instead the delicate suggestion, veiled hint, and mild allusions of their traditional aesthetic.

Between *Imotose kagami* and *Matsu no uchi* lay two years of intense work and study. In this short space of time, Tsubouchi started a voluminous political allegory, published four sizable literary translations and two novels. The first of these novels, *Kokoya kashiko* (Here and There), he left unfinished. It was being published in the *Eiri Chōya shinbun* and he had written fifteen chapters that appeared almost daily from March 20 to May 14, 1887. Saganoya Omuro, a younger writer living in Tsubouchi's house, wrote a favorable review of it that appeared in another paper. The editor of the *Chōya shinbun*, while paying a call at Tsubouchi's house, playfully remarked on clever authors who had their works touted in the press. Tsubouchi brooded about the comment for some time and then, pleading illness, returned the money paid him for completing the novel.

Kokoya kashiko is the story of a sixteen-year-old boy who, left impoverished by the death of his father, goes back and forth between Tokyo and Nagoya trying to make his way in a cruel world. Tsubouchi had been reading Dickens' novels about young people and had hoped to write of a boy who succeeds despite all the forces that oppose him. He abandoned the story at the point when his hero was beginning to study with the financial backing of a stranger who takes pity on him.

The second novel during this period, *Tanehiroi* (Seed Picking), appeared in the *Yomiuri shinbun* from October 1 to November 9, 1887. It is a fictional account of an incident that might have happened during a trip the author actually took in the summer of 1887. The author, traveling by steamship and train, overhears a man and woman talking. It seems that they had once been sweethearts and she tells him the sad tale of the misadventures that have befallen her with other men in the many years since they last met. The author later reads in the paper that she was arrested for attacking with a knife the man who had fathered her child, but had been released and was working as a maid in Osaka. It is a painfully contrived plot and loses much of its potential force in the confusion that results from its elaborate superstructure. Neither *Kokoya kashiko* nor *Tanehiroi* are of sufficient literary merit to justify an extensive examination, but both provided Tsubouchi with an opportunity to practice the style he was to develop more fully in his last two novels.

Chapter Five

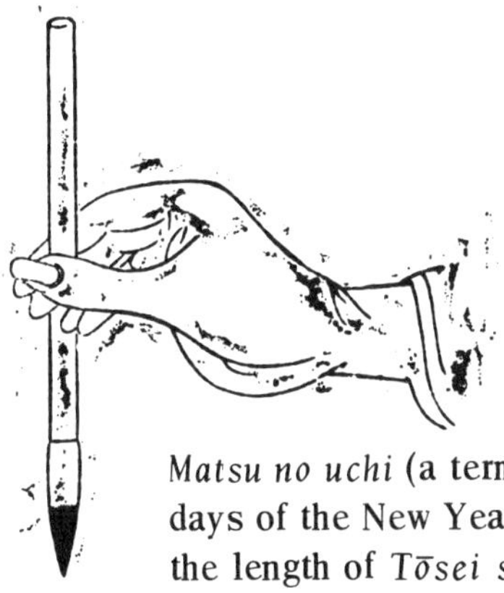

Matsu no uchi (a term referring to the first seven days of the New Year), a slight work just one-third the length of *Tōsei shosei katagi*, appeared in the *Yomiuri shinbun* from January 5 to February 8, 1888. Tsubouchi gathered some of the material for this story while on a trip to Atami with Sen shortly after their marriage. Its critical reception was both limited and negative; Tsubouchi seems once again to have failed to recapture the regard of his audience. He was obviously trying his hand at a very limited psychological study, apparently hoping to adapt psychological realism to the Japanese idiom by introducing slapstick and humor, even ridicule, into his handling of the plot. The experiment is certainly worthy of attention but must be considered a failure for it is a very silly little novel indeed. It is only through a detailed recapitulation of the story that we can see precisely what went wrong, for it becomes patently clear that Tsubouchi was unable to blend the ribald humor characteristic of Tokugawa and early Meiji fiction with a serious study of a sensitive young man's personality. While some of the scenes of mistaken identity and nighttime diversions take on an almost Mozartian flavor, there is none of the compensating sense of tragedy that makes the grand operas so memorable.

The story relates the events of the first seven days of the New Year 1888 in the life of a twenty-one-year-old student named Kazama Senzaburō. To expand the action somewhat the author appended a prologue concerning events four years earlier. There is little drama to the story and only a limited amount of suspense; it is rather a study of how Senzaburō's mind reacts to various suspicions he harbors against some of the other characters. He mistakenly believes that the wife of his benefactor, Kirimoto, is a former geisha named Kimihachi, and that she is attempting to seduce him or is at least involved in some sort of amorous relationship with a servant. The reader is also kept in the dark and does not know until almost the end of the novel that it is a case of mistaken identity, and that there is no connection between Mrs. Kirimoto and the geisha Kimihachi.

The prologue takes place in a teahouse where a group of students is having an uproarious party to celebrate the end of the year. Senzaburō, then a youth of seventeen, is ill in the washroom while his friend Miyaguchi[1] stands outside giving advice. Miyaguchi, four years Senzaburō's senior, affects great knowledge of how to fight off alcoholic nausea. This is the first time Senzaburō has attended such a party and he is furious at having been forced to drink against his will. As he staggers from the washroom, the geisha Kimihachi, whom the author describes as being somewhere between sixteen and nineteen, appears and is persuaded to help Senzaburō back upstairs to the party. She pushes and pulls, holding him tightly to get him on his way. Her efforts are the subject of derision from the other members of the group who have emerged to watch the procession on the stairs. The group includes two students named Hayashi and Onoda who are also several years older than Senzaburō.

After Senzaburō leaves the party, Kimihachi asks Hayashi about the young man and his brother. He describes Senzaburō as

[1] Continuing his practice from earlier novels, Tsubouchi refers to all the male characters by their family names. Here, however, he fails to give personal names of any but the hero. The women are, as usual, called by their given names, but Kirimoto's wife is not named.

a remote, unsociable fellow who has few if any close friends. Miyaguchi is able to give Kimihachi Senzaburō's address and she extracts a promise from Hayashi to take her there some time. In exchange she gives him a photograph of herself, which he demands as payment.

In the final part of the prologue we find Hayashi and Miyaguchi staggering home late at night, puzzling as they go over what could have attracted the geisha to Senzaburō. Hayashi is certain that Senzaburō will fall in love with the geisha at the slightest suggestion of interest on her part since he is so inexperienced with women, and he feels this will help the boy become more amiable. He plans to use the photo to keep the image of Kimihachi alive in Senzaburō's mind.

The main body of the novel is divided into twenty-eight very short chapters. It opens in the hot springs resort of Atami on the first of January, four years after the time of the prologue. Kirimoto, a man in his early thirties and the head of a prosperous household, is staying at an elegant inn with his wife and his elderly, retired father. From the conversation between husband and wife we learn that Senzaburō is now a part of their household, as is a fourteen-year-old girl named Omino, the orphaned daughter of wealthy relatives. They also have a groom in his early twenties and two maids. All the members of this complex household have been left at home in Tokyo while the master, mistress, and his father are in Atami. Because they are worried about having left Omino alone with two young men—that is with Senzaburō and the groom—Kirimoto and his wife decide that she will go back to Tokyo and send Omino to take her place in Atami. Mrs. Kirimoto arrives at her home in Tokyo the evening of the second.

At this point we learn that Senzaburō, also an orphan, had been supported by his clever but unscrupulous elder brother until the latter had been arrested and jailed. Left without the means to complete his education, he would have been destitute were it not for the intervention of Kirimoto, a distant relation. Senzaburō is very bookish and his aloofness makes him the object of ridicule by Omino and the maids. Knowledgeable in European studies, he frequently seeks moral support and wisdom from Bacon and Johnson.

Despite his restrained bearing, we learn that he has been nursing an infatuation for the geisha Kimihachi all these years since the night she had so casually embraced him at the teahouse. As his friends predicted, the photograph of Kimihachi has become inordinately important to him. Upon arriving at the Kirimoto home he takes the mistress to be Kimihachi for they strongly resemble each other and thinks Mrs. Kirimoto is just pretending she does not know him. He has made no reference to their supposed earlier meeting and she of course has given no sign that she recognizes him, but he is suspicious of everything she does and consistently judges her behavior in terms of her supposed background in the licensed quarter. The reader is not informed of Senzaburō's mistake and believes with him that Mrs. Kirimoto is the former geisha Kimihachi.

On the morning of the third, with the scene set back in the Tokyo house, Senzaburō is discovered taking a traditional cup of New Year's wine with the mistress along with the other members of the household. As the servants leave one by one, Senzaburō becomes more and more uncomfortable. He is habitually very awkward in the presence of women and is made even more so by his suspicions. He finds some reference to their earlier meeting in everything Mrs. Kirimoto says and is startled when she laughingly asks him if he knows Miyaguchi. He of course takes this as a hint on her part to remind him of the party at the teahouse, since Miyaguchi had also been there. As he gropes for a reply, the maid announces the arrival of Hayashi, who has come to pay a call on Senzaburō.

Hayashi had left school the previous year to take a job in the government, and since he and Senzaburō are of very different temperaments, neither young man had since contacted the other. Senzaburō thinks of Hayashi as crude and unprincipled, and cannot imagine why he has come. Does he too suspect that Mrs. Kirimoto is Kimihachi? Actually Hayashi merely wants to ask if

Senzaburō knows where their mutual friend Miyaguchi is staying in Atami for Hayashi is going to the resort the next day and would like to stay with him. Senzaburō does not know Miyaguchi's whereabouts but, undaunted, Hayashi proceeds to lecture him on "the law of taking a virgin." Relieved at finding Hayashi behaving in his usual vulgar manner, Senzaburō does not even argue with him although he finds the subject of his discourse offensive. Senzaburō's suspicions are aroused again however when Hayashi becomes excited at the sound of the mistress' voice calling the maid from her room.

Why, Senzaburō wonders, has the mistress returned so abruptly and why have they arranged to send Omino to Atami with an old family retainer named Kyūhachi? Does the mistress have designs on Senzaburō himself or has she some other plot in mind? Confused by his own suspicions, he even questions why the mistress leaves the house in the evening when as it happens she is just going to the bath.

Later, the mistress comes to Senzaburō's room, perfumed from the bath, and appearing very seductive to the young man. He is disappointed when he learns she has just come to ask him to accompany Omino to Atami. Old Kyūhachi who was to go has taken ill and his elderly wife will be sent instead, but she is a provincial Tokyoite and has never even been on a train. The mistress therefore wants Senzaburō to guide them.

Feeling relatively free of worry, Senzaburō is just about to set out for Atami the next day, the fourth, when he runs into the groom Kōgorō at the gate. As they exchange bows, Senzaburō begins to wonder why he was sent instead of Kōgorō. Is there perhaps a reason to suspect the mistress and the young, attractive groom?

The trip itself is a comedy of errors. To get from Tokyo to Atami, they must board a train at Shinbashi station at 10:30, change at Yokohama for one going to Kōzu where they will then get a boat for the balance of their journey. While on the train going from Shinbashi to Yokohama, Senzaburō catches sight of Hayashi. He had been so deeply engrossed in his own thoughts he had failed to remember that Hayashi was also going to Atami that day. Horrified at what Hayashi might say to Omino and how he might behave, Senzaburō contrives to duck around corners to avoid being seen and leads the women to the third-class waiting room although they have a first-class ticket. As he darts about trying to locate the first-class waiting room, he hears a whistle and realizes that in his confusion they have missed the train.

Omino gracefully suggests they go somewhere for lunch and stroll the promenade along the port while waiting for the next train. Although she is kind to him, Senzaburō is inarticulate as they dine and manages to spill tea on himself and knock his chopsticks onto the old woman's tray when he tries to wipe up. In his anxiety not to miss the next train, he leads them back to the station at 2:30 for a 3:30 departure. As he agonizes over his clumsiness and ineptitude, who should appear but Hayashi and, of course, there is no way to avoid his riding in the same compartment with them. Hayashi, it seems, had decided at the last minute not to take the earlier train but to call on their old school friend Onoda who lives in Yokohama. Finding him away, Hayashi had returned for the afternoon train.

This leg of the journey proves a terrible ordeal for Senzaburō. Hayashi chatters incessantly, his talk filled with flirtatious hints for Omino and thinly veiled insults directed at Senzaburō. He makes much of their having missed the first train and arriving so early for the next one.

They arrive in Kōzu too late to complete their journey and stay at an inn. In the bath, Hayashi discovers Onoda, for whom he had been searching in Yokohama. Onoda is also on his way to Atami. A notorious drinker and perpetrator of practical jokes, Onoda sees a rare opportunity in the discomfort of Senzaburō and quickly joins the party.

As they all dine together, Onoda becomes offensively drunk and embarrasses everyone. Senzaburō is particularly disturbed by his vulgarity and is furthermore greatly concerned that Onoda will say something about his earlier meeting with the geisha Kimihachi whom he of course still believes to be Mrs. Kirimoto.

Even Hayashi finally begins to weary of Onoda and warns Senzaburō that Onoda will surely try to carry off some sort of joke while they are sleeping. Hayashi promises to help Senzaburō keep watch during the night.

Onoda, however, almost immediately falls into a heavy drunken sleep, and Senzaburō decides there is no cause for concern. The lamp in their room burns out as he goes to the toilet. When he returns he tries to waken Hayashi, who has gone to sleep despite his earlier promise. He reaches into the covers to stir Hayashi and is greeted by a woman's screams.

We later learn that Onoda had awakened to find Senzaburō gone, opened the sliding doors between the rooms, and moved his bedding and the sleeping Hayashi to the other room, meanwhile shifting the women into their room and putting out the other light. The old woman had actually been awake the whole time, but thinking him a thief, had kept silent. Her bedding had been placed in reverse to the way Hayashi faced and so she had been utterly terrified when groping fingers pulled at her feet.

The next morning Senzaburō persuades the women to leave the inn and travel separately from Hayashi and Onoda. Although not fully understanding what has happened, Omino accepts Senzaburō's judgment, and the two are actually drawn closer together by the tomfoolery than they might otherwise have been. She later tells the old woman that she finally realized what a fine person Senzaburō was when they began to speak more openly to one another. She finds she has come to agree with the mistress's opinion that he is an unusually intelligent and sensitive young man.

Meanwhile the action shifts to the inn at Atami and we find the elder Kirimoto, a man of sixty, drinking with a fifty-year-old woman we later discover is Miyaguchi's mother. They discuss their children and the problems of aging and soon the old man is very drunk. As she coquettishly urges him to drink more, he begins to babble incoherently. Just at this juncture Senzaburō, Omino, and the old servant woman arrive. Senzaburō quickly takes charge, sends the old woman back to her room, and attempts to calm the elder Kirimoto. He has Omino bring a glass of water; when she approaches the old man she discovers his false teeth on the floor and realizes at once why he has been carrying on so.

The younger Kirimoto urges Senzaburō to stay on in Atami with them until the end of the seven-day New Year holiday, adding that Senzaburō really has nothing to do in Tokyo, a remark that wounds the sensitive young man deeply. Asked to compose poems on scenery, Senzaburō demurs, offended to have his meager talents praised as if he were a child. While he is standing on a balcony overlooking the sea with Kirimoto, Senzaburō overhears Omino telling their old servant how she has grown to admire him. She suggests that she may ask him for help in English after they return to Tokyo. Senzaburō is overjoyed but his happiness is soon ended when he comes upon Hayashi, Omino, and the old woman in a shop. Hayashi is bantering suggestively with Omino; he admires her new adult hair style and claims to have invented an even better one. She urges him to teach her how to do it and after considerable byplay, they speak of meeting the next day.

Senzaburō is nearly distraught at the idea of Omino seeing Hayashi. As he lies awake that night trying to decide how to warn Omino against Hayashi, it comes to him that he may have fallen in love with Omino himself, and that if he speaks about him to her father he may be accused of being jealous. Time is short since he is to depart for Tokyo in the morning.

The next day is very trying for Senzaburō. The Kirimotos and their servant remain in their rooms awaiting a planned excursion and he cannot get Omino alone long enough to speak to her. Finally she goes downstairs to wash and he asks her to join him in one of the many empty rooms vacated by guests now ending their holiday. He sternly tries to introduce the subject of her meeting with Hayashi, but she cannot understand what he means since she did not take Hayashi at all seriously. Senzaburō stubbornly refuses to name names.

Meanwhile Onoda and Hayashi are occupying another downstairs room, and at this point the reader learns for the first time that Mrs. Kirimoto and the geisha Kimihachi are two different people. Their friend Miyaguchi, who *also* had harbored an infatuation for Kimihachi over the years, had similarly mistaken Mrs. Kirimoto for Kimihachi just a few days before at the hot spring. When he realized his error, he, his mother, and the Kirimotos became friends.

While Onoda and Hayashi are talking, they also reveal to the reader that Kimihachi had been infatuated with Senzaburō's brother for many years, which accounts for her asking about Senzaburō the night of the New Year's party. Not knowing he had been arrested, she had been searching for him for some time. Since discovering his whereabouts, Kimihachi had been sending Senzaburō's brother things to make his life in prison more comfortable.

None of this is heard by Senzaburō who is still trying to make himself understood by Omino. He speaks to her of a devil trying to destroy her virtue but she continues to press him for a name. The sound of men's laughter comes to them and Senzaburō gets up and storms out of the room. The chapter ends with "Ah, truth and virtue are the seeds of laughter. Is there no justice in this world? Poor Kazama Senzaburō!"

Kirimoto receives a letter from Tokyo saying that there are now too few people in the house, and urging that Senzaburō return at once. Again flooded with suspicion, Senzaburō is back in Tokyo by nightfall to find the mistress smiling and the groom gone. After struggling for some time, he finally summons up the courage to ask her why Kōgorō had been dismissed. She explains that the groom had made improper advances. Some time before, he had apparently taken her casualness for personal interest and she had had to put him off by being very cold. Then he had turned to Omino and that was why she sent the girl to Atami. With her husband away, Kōgorō had wrongly imagined his mistress to be lonely and vulnerable.

Somewhat relieved at last, Senzaburō goes to bed. Just then a letter arrives from Senzaburō's brother, telling him that the charges against him have been dropped and that he has been released. He asks Senzaburō to meet him the next day at the home of Kimihachi, the geisha.

Thus the novel ends; we may assume Senzaburō will now understand his mistake regarding his mistress' identity, and realize what the reader already knows.

* * * * * * *

It is apparent that a great many changes occurred in Tsubouchi's novelistic technique in the two years that elapsed between *Imotose kagami* and *Matsu no uchi*. In this later book, we find not a single protracted moralistic digression; in fact, the author's tone is one of bemused objectivity. He continues to make remarks about the characters and events, but they are more in the nature of a running commentary than a statement of a serious moral code. As we have seen, the plot is quite straightforward and, except for one flashback on the trip from Shinbashi to Yokohama, the time sequence is surprisingly consistent. We are no longer wafted into long histories of events in the lives of various characters. While there are again scenes that slice a piece of action in two, as when Senzaburō's attempt to warn Omino is interrupted by the dialogue between Onoda and Hayashi, they are much less painful to read.

In part the reader is less troubled by this and other breaks in the plot line because the whole story is so insignificant. In the process of simplifying the plot, Tsubouchi has also reduced the intensity of the relations between the characters to the point where it is hard to muster interest in what happens. From the first, it is apparent that Senzaburō misinterprets the events going on around him; the only suspense is derived from the question of how Kimihachi, if indeed it is she, has made such a good marriage. But Senzaburō does not address himself to this point and so there is no discussion of it.

Recent critical interest in *Matsu no uchi* has focused on Tsubouchi's handling of Senzaburō's thoughts and the novel has been seen as a superior example of the psychological realism Tsubouchi advocated in *Shōsetsu shinzui*.[2] It is apparent that the author made every effort to stay within the narrowest possible confines, restricting his story to seven fixed days, and his characters to only a few. However, the truth is that it does not really matter—to the reader or to the characters—if Senzaburō's suspicions are correct. It is fascinating to see a very weak or a very strong mind at work, but Senzaburō belongs to neither extreme. He is an ordinary man in the same sense that Misawa Tatsuzō of *Imotose kagami* is, but Tatsuzō is engaged in making critical decisions that will affect his whole life and the lives of others. Senzaburō is pictured at a very inconclusive moment in his career and little changes in the course of the seven days. He grows closer to Omino and there are intimations of continued friendship, but all this is achieved with little strain. Were he wracked by indecision or torn by doubt, we might be more concerned, but as it is his feelings are on a fairly superficial plane and our interest is limited. We are sorry for him, as one always is for a shy or nervous person, and we are amused by the way he bumbles about, but we cannot be overly concerned.

There are striking similarities between this novel and Futabatei's *Ukigumo*. The chronology clearly demonstrates that Futabatei used *Matsu no uchi* as a working model for *Ukigumo*; the most striking analogies between the two books occur in the latter portions of *Ukigumo* written months after *Matsu no uchi* was published. In this case the comparison only serves to demonstrate more vividly the weaknesses of Tsubouchi's novel. Futabatei's hero Bunzō is made completely wretched by his cousin Osei's treatment; she breaks his will by her indifference and distorts his reason by her every action. Omino in this novel by contrast is barely a personality at all; she is, in fact, as vapid as Oyuki in *Imotose kagami*. One has the impression of a sweet, rather tactful girl just becoming aware that men exist. She is playful and pleasant with the servants, and sensible with the adults. But we know almost nothing else about her and certainly cannot predict her

[2] Inagaki Tatsurō, "Kaidai," *Tsubouchi Shōyō shū*. In *Meiji bungaku zenshū*, 16: 396; Kawatake Shigetoshi and Yanagida Izumi, *Tsubouchi Shōyō*, pp. 173–75.

future development. Senzaburō is as stern in his moral judgments as Bunzō but the consequences of his rigidity are so slight that this quality merely becomes a source of amusement.

In fact the reader is more amused by Senzaburō than engrossed in his mind. This is perhaps why the novel fails. It is impossible to take seriously a young man who thinks himself in love with a woman because she once touched him and who clings to her memory through a photograph for four years. Even given the segregated nature of Meiji society, this degree of romanticism is difficult to accept. The humorous characters—Hayashi, Onoda, and Miyaguchi—are carry-overs from *Tōsei shosei katagi*, stock figures in a youthful comedy. They have no particular dimension and their only function is to amuse. The groom, the maids, even the old servant, are pasteboard figures set on the stage to play their minor roles. Kirimoto is not memorable, his wife is barely more real; the older Kirimoto almost emerges as a person in the scene where he loses his teeth but he is all too soon lost to us again. Everything is pleasantly humorous from the foibles of the hero to the bedroom farce perpetrated by his friends.

In all, we do not know enough about anyone to react very strongly and what we do know is simply not convincing. The situation is too frivolous for serious events to emerge and the characterization too vapid. There is not a single memorable scene; none of the impact of *Imotose kagami* is here.

As we have suggested above, there is a real possibility that Tsubouchi was attempting to combine the farcical humor of premodern Japanese fiction with some of the novelistic techniques of the Western world. This might possibly account for the critical and popular failure of the novel. The reading public would most likely not be bothered by such slapstick as the switching of the bedding in the inn; however the average reader and certainly the critic would be greatly troubled by the use of such foolishness in conjunction with any more somber theme. The story is out of phase both internally and with Tsubouchi's avowed goals in writing fiction. There is no point in attempting a realistic novel—which is after all what this is despite the instances of mistaken identity and accidental meetings with old friends—unless the author is trying to probe some important area of human behavior. In *Imotose kagami* Tsubouchi showed every sign of understanding this essential point, but here he seems to have lost his grip on the idea and let himself revert to the safety of the kind of slapstick his predecessors had so frequently depended upon.

A similar confusion of focus besets the opening chapters of Futabatei's *Ukigumo*. His hero too is bungling, awkward, and weak, and many of the early scenes are more humorous than pathetic. Futabatei, however, seems to have grasped the meaning of the human dilemma more firmly, and was able to salvage his novel by carrying his introspection to a more significant depth. He hinges his story on a true crisis—the loss of his hero's position and the subsequent effect of this on his domestic life—and thus avoids the superficiality of the plot of *Matsu no uchi*. The two novels are in many ways strikingly similar and yet they are aeons apart because of this very point. One feels that this must be what Tsubouchi meant when he said he could never be as good a writer as Futabatei. The two men were both trying to write a true modern realistic novel at almost exactly the same time, each obviously strongly influencing the other in every way, but it was Futabatei who had the critical and popular success.

One particular similarity to *Ukigumo* should be noted, for while it is a minor point, it sheds some light on the problem of whether or not Futabatei's *Ukigumo* is a finished novel. Futabatei's contemporaries accepted it as complete, but in 1937 the critic Yanagida Izumi believed that he found evidence that proved it to be unfinished. His evidence has since been discredited but the impression that *Ukigumo* is incomplete still lingers in the minds of some. They offer as their argument the open-endedness of the novel, for it closes with Bunzō, almost like Scarlett O'Hara, ascending the stairs to await another day. *Matsu no uchi* ends in almost identical fashion, with very similar words. Remembering that this novel was written at least eighteen months before the final chapters of *Ukigumo*, we can easily imagine that Futabatei found nothing inappropriate in his inconclusive but highly pregnant final line.

Since writing *Imotose kagami* Tsubouchi had been struggling to "modernize" his style, that is to create some kind of linguistic medium to express realistic fiction. He had felt from the first that a new language was necessary for a modern literature but devising such a language proved an extremely difficult matter. This effort occupied the energies of many of his contemporaries and each reached a solution that was different in some respect from the other. Tsubouchi's style as it evolved by the time he wrote *Matsu no uchi* is one that is essentially more prosaic—that is, more like prose in the Western sense—than the poetic style of his first two novels. There is far more use of straightforward sentences that convey exactly what is meant, and far less reliance on decorative, allusive language. The grammatical inflections are those of *bungo-tai* or classical Japanese, but this style should not be confused with the one he had used earlier. It is essentially a language of direct communication and is markedly different from the premodern language of fictional narrative that was vague, suggestive, inconclusive, and invited a variety of interpretations for any given expression. In other words, more or less direct exposition has replaced the traditional narrative diction that was comparable to operatic recitative. The words themselves as distinguished from their inflections are essentially those of Tsubouchi's own time and do not seem archaic or anachronistic. Most of the nouns, verbs, and adjectives are basically the same as those of the spoken language, although the inflections used in this text are found only in writing.

In the process of creating this new language for fiction, much has been lost. The diction of *Matsu no uchi* is flat and colorless; even the dialogue lacks the sparkle of Tsubouchi's first novels. All the music of the traditional 7–5 or 8–6 syllabic rhythm is gone and we are left with a thumping, monotonous prose. When Tsubouchi first entered upon the discussion of how to modernize the written language to make it appropriate for composing realistic fiction, he was troubled by the consequences of sacrificing the traditional lyrical narrative for something more readily communicable. *Matsu no uchi* demonstrates rather vividly how justified his fears were. In the process of clarifying his prose, eliminating ambiguities and unnecessary verbiage, he has also taken away all the poetry. While one welcomes the absence of digressions in heavy rhetorical language, one misses the variety and texture they brought to his style.

This was perhaps a necessary if unfortunate step in the transition from one style to another. Within a few years, a literary style notable for cleanness of line began to appear in novels, but Tsubouchi, weaned as he was on the Tokugawa literature, was not the person to develop it.

The critic Ishibashi Ningetsu shared our disappointment about *Matsu no uchi*. Writing in *Kokumin no tomo* in October 1888, he expressed his chagrin that the author of *Tōsei shosei katagi* and *Imotose kagami* should have produced such a banal work. The novel, he declared, has no plot and no structure, and the low level of much of its humor is painful to behold. When will Tsubouchi create a hero who is not a neurotic weakling? Surely normal people have some place in modern fiction, he asserted. In all Ishibashi was shocked that the man who had been accepted as the leading figure in the revitalization of Japanese fiction should sink so low.[3]

[3] "*Nisegane tsukai, Matsu no uchi*," *Kokumin no tomo*, no. 31 (October 1888), pp. 38–39.

Chapter Six

Tsubouchi's last serious attempt to write realistic fiction was a short work called *Saikun* (The Wife), which he labored over for more than a month between October and November 1888. The influence of Futabatei's personality on Tsubouchi was strongest at just this time. The younger man's habitual severe self-criticism caused Tsubouchi to scrutinize his art in every detail. Tsubouchi, who had begun writing fiction in his early twenties with the greatest pleasure, dashing off chapter after chapter, now agonized over every line, struggling to modernize his style, his plot, and his characterization. The whole experience unnerved him. In January 1889 he vowed never again to write a novel with the intention of selling it.

Saikun is a well-wrought novel. Tsubouchi has employed his dexterity with plot to its best advantage. The pieces of the story fit neatly together and the characters interact upon each other in a way new to Tsubouchi's fiction. It is a very successful story and should have received considerable critical attention.

Unfortunately it was published in the 1889 New Year's supplement of the intellectual magazine *Kokumin no tomo* in the same issue with Yamada Bimyō's *Kochō*. Bimyō was another of the young authors striving to revitalize Japanese fiction. It was the illustration for *Kochō* rather than the story that attracted so much attention. Critics and public alike were jolted by the partly nude woman pictured in the magazine. Tsubouchi's novel, on which he had lavished such care, passed relatively unnoticed.

Saikun is a more moving story than *Matsu no uchi*, penetrating into those hidden areas of human behavior and response where reason plays little part. It deals once again with the same cast of characters we have become so familiar with in Tsubouchi's novels; the upper-class intellectual young bureaucrat, this time identical with the weakling who squanders money on women; his educated wife, somehow out of step with Japanese life; her caustic stepmother and sweet bumbling father, neither able to help her when she most needs them. *Saikun*, however, is enhanced by the way Tsubouchi has presented one of the servants, an apprentice maid named Osono. Naïve, overly trusting, limited in her knowledge and understanding, Osono falls victim to the cruelty and indifference of everyone surrounding her, rich and poor alike, until in the end she is destroyed by the very system she reveres.

The story opens as Osono is contemplating her good fortune at being placed in the Shimokōbe house. In her previous position she had been the only servant in a boardinghouse with eighteen paying guests and had been forced to work incredibly long hours for a miserly salary. Here the family consists only of the Shimokōbe couple, Sadao and Otane, and his elderly mother. To serve them there is, in addition to herself, a cook, a rickshaw man and his wife, a resident student, and a distant relative whose sole function is to care for the old woman. In Osono's eyes, everyone seems gentle and kind. Even the cook, who has a sharp tongue and is prone to gossip, offers no real obstacle, and for the first time in her young life she is praised for her efforts.

Osono had been orphaned some two years before, and she had been left in the care of an unscrupulous aunt who thought only of how she could use the girl to get some money. Her aunt regularly pockets Osono's small earnings. At fourteen, the girl craves affection of any kind, and is grateful for the few moments of attention her mistress gives her. As she goes to sleep at night in the cramped maid's room off the kitchen, Osono prays that she may go on working in this splendid household forever.

Things are not really going well in the family. The cook is fired abruptly, and before she leaves she tries to tell Osono what a wastrel Sadao is and how Otane, for all her education, knows nothing about managing a household. Sadao has a new concubine, she reports, and has had to pay a tremendous sum to rid himself of another girl. Osono can see how the tradesmen are pressing for payment of their bills and she learns she must carefully screen visitors before admitting them to the house. She notes how frequently Sadao is away and how strained things are between him and his wife. There are no open quarrels, however, and the quiet and restraint of the family are quite sufficient to earn Osono's admiration.

Unknown to anyone, Otane has decided to leave her husband. She has learned of Sadao's latest exploits, but she herself realizes that this is not the real reason she wants to go back to her father's house; she is not able to truly understand why she is so unhappy. Otane had never really wanted to marry, disdaining the traditional role of a wife, but had never really intended to seek a career either, although she had gone through normal school. Her classmates had thought her unlikely to make a good match and were sure she should not succeed as a wife. How jealous they had been when, at twenty-two, Otane had become betrothed to Sadao, a brilliant young man five years her senior. Sadao soon became famous among government servants, and a year after their marriage, was sent to England where he lived three years. His books began to appear and were widely read. Otane flourished in reflected glory until, after his return, she realized that he was no longer at all interested in her as a woman.

As Otane sits contemplating leaving her husband, her stepmother Okumi comes to ask her for the very considerable sum of forty yen. Okumi's son Yoshi, Otane's half-brother, has managed to acquire this sizable debt in some unspecified illegal manner, and if it is not repaid he will be imprisoned. At the end of the previous year, Yoshi had presented his parents with a hundred yen debt of which Sadao had generously paid half. The remaining half was to have been paid in monthly installments but Yoshi had been pocketing the money his mother turned over to him each month. Now not only has the remaining fifty-yen debt come due, but this new forty yen has been added to the total. Otane's father is retired from the government service and the family is living in a far more modest fashion than it had in Otane's girlhood. They manage on a monthly allowance Sadao gives them added to a modest sum her father earns as a teacher in an extension school. They can ill afford Yoshi's wastefulness, but they have continued to indulge him and hope Sadao will step in again.

Otane explains that she cannot ask Sadao for the money because of certain domestic difficulties. Okumi does not believe her and feels that her stepdaughter resents the way they pamper Yoshi. Okumi leaves in a fury and visits various other relatives trying in vain to borrow the money. Otane in the meanwhile goes to her father's house and attempts to broach the subject of a divorce. He is very kind but quite unable to catch the drift of her delicate hints; she is just about to thrust her feelings upon him more forcefully when Okumi returns. A student comes to take her father to his class and Otane turns to her stepmother, trying again to explain her problems. Okumi barely listens to her words and abruptly dismisses the idea of a divorce as the whimperings of a spoiled child. All Japanese men have affairs, she asserts, and it is only you foolish modern girls who find them any problem. It is their right, indeed their obligation. This is what all education results in, she concludes.

Otane returns home, determined to stay on with Sadao for her father's sake, if for no other reason. Were she to be divorced, his main source of income would be cut off and she could not hope to earn enough as a teacher to compensate for it all. She is conscious, too, of what people would say were she to leave her husband; no one had expected her to make a decent wife and she would be proving them correct. But how is she to raise the money for Yoshi? That evening her husband spends one of his rare nights at home, but as is usually the case he is accompanied by a crowd of friends who remain until late. Otane can hardly be expected to talk seriously with Sadao as he stretches out beside her that night, lost in a drunken stupor.

By the afternoon of the next day Otane has decided to raise the money herself. She reviews the list of people on whom she might rely for help in such a crisis and realizes there is virtually no one. Finally, lacking any other alternative, she calls the maid Osono to her room and asks her to take three summer kimonos to a pawnshop and get forty yen for them. Osono, more sophisticated in such matters than her mistress, says that while she knows of a shop where her aunt deals, she would not be able to get such a large sum without a passbook. The girl suggests that she might borrow a passbook from her aunt. Otane is reluctant to involve anyone else and asks her to try for thirty yen instead. The pawnbroker tells the girl that he will allow only eighteen yen on the kimonos and also insists that they produce a passbook. A gardener named Seigorō who frequents her aunt's house overhears this discussion and agrees to go for her aunt's passbook. Meanwhile Osono returns to ask her mistress if it would be all right to take only eighteen yen. Otane reluctantly searches out two more kimonos and asks Osono to try to raise at least twenty-five yen in all.

Osono is gone a long time; Otane begins to fear she had been mistaken in trusting her with such a large sum of money. In her anxiety, she is cold to the point of rudeness to her mother-in-law.

We next find Osono, nearly distraught, being questioned by a policeman. Someone has stolen the twenty-five yen she got from the pawnbroker. We learn that she had waited a long time for Seigorō to return with the passbook. Finally, at nine o'clock, a little urchin who lived next to her aunt had brought it saying that Seigorō had had to return to his own home and had sent the boy in his stead. Anxious to be on her way, Osono had thrust the money into her sash, barely heeding the warning of the pawnbroker to take great care on her return trip. In a deserted spot, she was set upon by a thief who escaped with the money despite her valiant attempts to stop him.

The policeman has a hard time persuading Osono to go home, fearful as she is of facing her mistress. He finally turns her over to the student at the gate, remarking as he does that so young a child should never have been sent out on such an errand at night. Just as he says this, Sadao returns, and hears of the theft.

Sadao is drunk. Otane had not expected him at all that evening, it being Saturday, a night he usually spent elsewhere, and she is utterly bewildered by his appearance at this juncture. He brushes by her and marches into the house without a word. Otane goes to the kitchen, looks in briefly on Osono, who is prostrate and babbling incoherently, and gets charcoal for her husband's hibachi. Otane leaves the kitchen without a word, while the newly hired cook sits beside the girl offering neither consolation nor sympathy.

When Sadao demands an explanation, Otane realizes she can do nothing but tell the truth, which she does with surprising humility and tact. Sadao is furious at the idea of her having stooped to dealing with a pawnbroker. She asks his forgiveness. Here is his response:

> You think all you have to do is apologize? Everything in this house is mine. Alright, so maybe some of it is yours, but still everyone thinks of us as one. If you do something vile, it's my scandal, my name that's ruined. You disgrace me like this and think you can get away with "I'm sorry"? What are you going to say when the police ask what the twenty-five yen was for and where she got it and what kind of money it was? What will you tell them? Shimōkobe has gone to a pawnshop. That's what they'll all be saying. It will all come back to me, the whole damn thing. It's absolutely beyond belief. You are utterly selfish. They say a little knowledge is a dangerous thing. In your selfish way

> you pick up some crazy ideas about "rights" and "personal property" and immediately you think these things are yours. What? You don't think so? Then why the hell did you go ahead and pawn them on your own without asking me? What? That's why you're apologizing? You think all you have to do is say you're sorry? Is that going to squelch all the rumors? What an idiotic idea! She's so damned ignorant and she goes sneaking around with her "rights" and "personal property." No wonder they say you can't teach women anything. I was in England a long time and I can tell you there's no such thing there, or in France, or in Germany. It's absolutely incredible. Not only does she grab things out of the house but she gets us into this mess. What? You're sorry? You're damn right you're sorry. What? You were going to talk it over with me? Then why the hell didn't you? You thought I'd say no? So what if I did! How the hell were you so sure anyway? Are you some kind of fortuneteller? That's what I want to know. Let me hear it. What? You needed the money in a big hurry? What? Because you didn't know when I'd be home? Wasn't I here last night? Why didn't you say something? Why didn't you talk it over with me? The whole thing makes no sense. You surely could have waited another day or another night. Why couldn't you wait 'til I got home? What? You thought I'd be away tonight? How could you be so sure? That's what I want to hear. Let me hear it. What? What's that about Saturday? I usually stay away Saturday? What the hell's wrong with that? What? You don't see anything wrong about it? Then why did you just say you did? You didn't? Didn't you just this minute say exactly that? The whole damn business makes no sense. Disgusting. Vile. Unspeakable.[1]

Otane does not defend herself. She has a great deal to say on

[1] *Shōyō senshū*, Bessatsu 1:859–60.

the subject of his guilt but she feels very much to blame for what has happened and remains silent.

Meanwhile, off in her own room, Osono hears Sadao's voice and, while she cannot make out the words, she realizes how angry he is. She can also hear Otane's apologetic tone and she is even more distraught than before. Unable to think of the proper action, she agonizes over the consequences of the theft. Will she be forced to make up the loss? Whan she worked at the boarding house, they made her pay back twenty-five sen[2] she had lost in the marketplace. But how can she ever repay twenty-five yen? Her monthly salary is only seventy sen. Overwhelmed at the mere dimensions of the problem, she creeps up to the room where Otane and Sadao are quarreling. She is in time to hear one final thrust from Sadao. "I don't want to hear any lectures from you. I know all about it. 'Women's rights' indeed! Selfish beasts! Carrying on like that. Bitch! I told you to shut up."[3]

Sadao goes to the entrance way and shouts for the student to call the rickshaw man. Soon he is off. It is one o'clock in the morning. Otane remains in the room where they quarreled, weeping inconsolably. Osono slides open the door and tries to speak to her. Bowing to the floor, Osono tearfully apologizes, but Otane remains as she is, her back turned, her face buried in her handkerchief. Osono comes close and speaks again. Infuriated, Otane lashes out: "I told you to get out of here. Shut that door." Osono retreats but cannot leave and tries to speak again. Otane cuts her off. "I told you to shut that door!" As Osono leaves, it finally comes to Otane that the girl was trying to apologize, but she is so absorbed with her own sorrow that she cannot find room for Osono's problems.

Otane realizes that Sadao has all but told her to get out. She decides she must leave before he has an opportunity to order her out, and put aside all considerations of her father's feelings and her reputation. She will go home and explain everything as soon as possible. Exhausted she falls asleep on the cushions.

2 There were one hundred sen in one yen.

3 *Shōyō senshū*, Bessatsu 1:861.

In the morning, Otane awakens and, with heavy heart, goes about opening the shutters. More determined than ever, she realizes that this is the day she must make an end to her marriage. Suddenly the cook rushes in and blurts out that Osono has drowned herself in the well.

In a brief postscript, the author adds that on December 8 of that year, Otane was divorced and returned to her father's house. Osono's aunt was arrested on suspicion of the theft but eventually released. It was Seigorō, the aunt's lover, who stole the money. The following year, Sadao remarried. His second wife was the concubine of whom the cook had spoken. She was a woman who had followed Sadao home from France.

* * * * * * *

The outstanding innovation in this novel is the way Tsubouchi shifts the central focus back and forward between Osono and Otane. A short novel approximately one-half the length of *Matsu no uchi*, *Saikun* is divided into four substantial chapters of almost equal length. The first chapter, entitled "The Maid and the Wife," is told entirely from Osono's point of view. While Tsubouchi occasionally uses her here as a vehicle for relaying information about the Shimokōbe family, on the whole he manages this subtly, and the reader is not distracted from his central purpose, which is to demonstrate Osono's youth and innocence. In this chapter, Otane approaches Osono and questions her briefly about her background. We see at once that Otane is not cruel or harsh, but she is certainly not warm or enthusiastic either; we also see how Osono seizes these tiny crumbs of kindness as great gifts.

The second chapter, "Parents and Children," is entirely about Otane and her visit to her father's house. Most of the content is conveyed by direct exchanges between Otane, her father, and her stepmother Okumi. The third chapter, "With Hesitation," is less direct and, consequently, less forceful than the first two. Here Tsubouchi seeks to fill in an array of background information. The chapter tends to wordiness and there is a fair amount of repetition of information about Otane and Sadao that the reader has already surmised from earlier discussions. Tsubouchi also occasionally interjects personal comments, thereby further distracting the reader from the central issues. In the last four pages of the chapter we return to a direct narration of the events as Otane goes about sending Osono to the pawnbroker. The chapter ends with Otane awaiting Osono's return late in the evening.

The fourth and final chapter, "Confusion," opens with the policeman questioning Osono. In choosing to launch into the action in this highly dramatic fashion, Tsubouchi sacrificed the impact he might have achieved by a direct narration of the events leading to the theft and had to settle for relating them in retrospect, beginning with a rather contrived "If you were to ask what has happened to Osono. . . ." The remainder of the chapter, however, is quite compelling and there is a genuinely skillful handling of the interplay between Otane's reactions, her quarrel with Sadao, and Osono's agonized thoughts culminating in the exchange between Osono and Otane as the girl tries to obtain her mistress's forgiveness. From then on until the last few lines, we are entirely within Otane's mind.

Tsubouchi seems to have come to an important realization regarding the kind of introspective fiction he was hoping to write; if he entered the minds of several of his characters he would enrich his story, giving it a dimension it had been lacking. He presents his characters at a moment of real crisis, thereby avoiding the air of superficiality that dominated *Matsu no uchi*. He has limited his comments in most of the story and, except for the third chapter, allows the characters' words, thoughts, and actions to speak instead.

A new quality of seriousness pervades *Saikun*. Even when Tsubouchi speaks, he does not use the flippant, sarcastic tone he had employed earlier. While one may regret the passing of the humor that had characterized *Tōsei shosei katagi*, there is no doubt that he had to stop inserting his sarcasm into his fiction if he was to create a unity of emotion within a single story. It just does not seem to have been possible for Tsubouchi to intersperse arch humor, slapstick and pathos all in one novel successfully. As we saw in *Matsu no uchi*, what had suffered was the serious side of the story; it had degenerated into melodrama. *Saikun* avoids the melodramatic, despite its outcome, by the restraint of its diction and the singularity of its plot line.

Otane is a cold woman, probably as self-centered as Sadao accuses her of being, but Tsubouchi makes it clear that her position is in a sense as pathetic as Osono's. She too is without anyone to whom to turn at a time of true necessity. Consider the situation: she is a woman of twenty-six, of respectable lineage and what passed for a good education, and yet she does not have access to any money of her own and must go to her husband for everything. She is not even willing to claim her right to her own clothes when he challenges her.

Sadao—brilliant though he is—is not above assuming the prerogatives of the traditional Japanese husband. He feels no compunction about being away whenever he likes without informing anyone and rarely exchanges civilized conversation with his wife. Of course he has no interest in her and, as it turns out, is deeply involved with a Frenchwoman. He could not easily have divorced Otane as soon as he would have liked for it would have caused a tremendous scandal. This was why he had to dismiss the cook when she accidentally found out about the woman. It was one thing to have a mistress in Meiji Japan, even possibly a European one, but quite another to divorce a Japanese wife for a European. In the end he did, which shows considerable strength of will, but he had in the meanwhile found an excellent excuse for ridding himself of Otane.

Otane herself wanted to get out of the marriage but felt trapped by various social pressures. Perhaps the whole business of the pawnbroker was an outgrowth of her desire to be finally repudiated by Sadao. One hesitates to speak of subconscious motivation in a Meiji novel, but it would seem that what we have here is not a turn of plot conveniently inserted to conclude a story, but rather a genuine sifting of alternatives by a character who proceeds from an irrational premise to an illogical conclusion from motives she herself does not suspect. There really was no reason why she could not wait to ask Sadao for the money, humiliating though it may have been, and it was an outrageous violation of her responsibilities as mistress to send Osono out after dark on such an errand.

The reader's greatest sympathy goes out to Osono. Somehow we do care about Osono despite the obvious appeal to our emotions; we care because it is her own voice that tells us of her situation and she is not a girl to feel sorry for herself. Her joy at the simplest pleasures throws the indifference of her mistress into even greater relief. She bears no ill will toward her aunt or to the cook who is disagreeable to her. She wants only to think the best of everyone in the Shimokōbe household and refuses to believe the gossip she hears. Osono is a nice girl and she is victimized in the worst possible way: by carelessness and indifference. Sadao does not even mention the danger she was exposed to when he harangues his wife; Otane cannot even muster the strength to extend a single word of kindness to her when she comes to apologize.

* * * * * * *

Saikun is a slight novel but it is a good one. It would rank among the best written in Japan in the 1880s. It is a serious piece of fiction clearly of a different class from the hundreds of others appearing in newspapers and magazines at this time. It is moving in the way only serious fiction can be and Tsubouchi is to be credited with having achieved the goal he set for himself while still a student. He had finally written a well-proportioned realistic novel that holds the reader's attention throughout.

Two reviews of *Saikun* appeared in subsequent issues of *Kokumin no tomo*. The first, by Fukuchi Genichirō, praised the brisk, direct narrative style. Fukuchi was deeply impressed by the degree of insensitivity the characters demonstrated toward the unfortunate Osono. He noted that the significance of Otane's lack of comprehension of her own problems had been lost on some readers; he found it a major strength of the novel.[4]

A longer review by Yoda Gakkai appeared the following

[4] "Harunoya shujin no *Saikun*," *Kokumin no tomo*, no. 39 (January 1889), p. 32.

month. Yoda was much disturbed by the fact that Osono killed herself because of such insensitive, immoral people. While conceding that a novel cannot be used as a handbook for teaching morality, he could not accept this turn of the plot as appropriate in any sense. Yoda, however, was impressed by the vividness of the presentation and the clever touches that helped to tie the elements of the story together. Even he had failed to realize that the woman referred to earlier in the story was a Frenchwoman until the very last line and he thought it was particularly moving that the insensitive Otane leaves Sadao's house wearing gloves Osono had knitted for her earlier in the novel. Such qualities did not seem to entirely outweigh certain minor plot flaws he discovered: for example, why did Otane send Osono on this dangerous errand when she might have sent the student living in their home?[5]

With the completion of *Saikun* in November of 1888 and an aborted attempt at one final political novel the following year, Tsubouchi turned his attention to the theater, a genre that would absorb much of his talent until his death. He seems to have given up the writing of fiction out of a sense of frustration. As we have noted above, he remarked that he decided in January 1889 that he would no longer write fiction "for profit," a phrase that Futabatei used again in July of the same year when he too decided to abandon the writing of fiction, in his case, as we have seen, to become a member of the government bureaucracy. It is tempting to speculate on what the two friends meant by this expression, for surely it must have had a special significance to them. In some part at least it must refer to the problems they were having in creating an audience for the kind of fiction they were writing. This was more pertinent an issue in Tsubouchi's case, for he was indeed having difficulty in gaining a favorable critical reaction to his work. The two brief reviews noted above were virtually the only contemporary notices of *Saikun* to appear, and since they were in the same publication in which the story

[5] "Harunoya-kun shōsetsu *Saikun*," *Kokumin no tomo*, no. 41 (February 1889), pp. 22–26.

was printed they might well have been solicited for that reason. *Matsu no uchi* also had aroused little critical attention, and that was decidedly negative. Futabatei had less cause to complain of critical neglect, but he too seemed to have felt that he was not appreciated by his contemporaries.

They might also have meant that they were unable to write a novel that would satisfy their intellectual standards and still interest the Japanese reading public. Both men were trying to write novels with popular appeal and seem not to have conceived of the possibility of an elitist literature. With the enormous reading public available to them they obviously hoped to succeed commercially as well as artistically. This would surely account in part at least for Tsubouchi's choice of a *katagi mono* for his first book and a "mirror book" for his second. It also must be the basic reason for the frivolity of *Matsu no uchi*. But this conception obviously had little to do with the artistic novel Tsubouchi had argued for in *Shōsetsu shinzui*. Both he and Futabatei must have become aware of the conflict inherent in trying to write a novel that would be both a popular and artistic success, although it was an entirely new concept in Japan where such a dichotomy had never been recognized.

We have no way of knowing if Tsubouchi himself realized how good *Saikun* was, particularly since it received so little critical attention. He seems to have found the writing of it an agony, if we may judge by the time it took him to compose it, and we may assume that a major part of his difficulty was again in finding a literary style that would satisfy his aesthetic sense and still seem "modern." Technically *Saikun* is quite similar in style to *Matsu no uchi*; again the words themselves are those of the contemporary language while the inflections are those of the literary style known as *bungo-tai*. In this latter novel, the diction is even more flat and monotonous than in *Matsu no uchi* for, in keeping with the more somber and direct presentation of the story in general, the author has avoided the deliberate ambiguities and facetiousness of his earlier story. The playfulness of *Matsu no uchi* had perhaps allowed Tsubouchi some stylistic pleasure even while writing in this new "modern" style, but *Saikun* is throughout far too serious to permit such leeway, and Tsubouchi may have genuinely found the straightforward diction demanded by the plot offensive to his sensibilities.

We can only view Tsubouchi's withdrawal from the world of fiction with regret for he had overcome many of his earlier difficulties by the time he wrote *Saikun* and had made substantial progress along the course he had set for himself. A sense of deeper understanding pervades this final novel. *Saikun* concerns itself with social criticism in the same sense as *Imotose kagami*, but everything about it bespeaks a maturity not present in the earlier book. The singularity of tone, unity of plot line, and tightness of diction are all indicative of the author's control over his material. It is as if out of all the confused heritage of Japanese fiction and theater, combined with his reading of Western fiction, Tsubouchi had at last isolated exactly what he required to write the kind of story he envisaged in *Shōsetsu shinzui*. Remembering that his critical essay had appeared only four years before *Saikun*, we can only admire the swiftness with which he achieved his goal, and wonder at his own failure to recognize the extent of his victory.

* * * * * * *

In this study it has been necessary to present four of Tsubouchi's novels in considerable detail to correct a whole series of misimpressions literary historians have passed on. The first and most striking of these is their repeated assertion that since *Tōsei shosei katagi* is not "modern" or "realistic" by most definitions, Tsubouchi had failed in his mission to create the novel he anticipated in *Shōsetsu shinzui*. Clearly he was trying in his first novel, but only barely trying, for he was much more involved in his massive plot than in developing the psychology of any one character or group of characters. But his efforts, no matter how tentative, to make fiction meaningful demand recognition even in this novel. Already in the character of the heroine Tanoji we have a subtly drawn young woman of strength and consistency, a woman who knows what she wants and will fight to get it. Her lover does not come through as a very attractive personality and his friends are interesting but not commanding. The influence of the theater is so strong in *Tōsei shosei katagi*, one feels almost as if Tsubouchi were writing a script for a play and not a novel at all. Set scenes abruptly shifting from plot to subplot and back without any true narrative transition, dialogue without background, and the most momentous events occurring offstage and lighthearted frivolity on—all these are techniques more suited to a play than a novel. Still there is more structured plot, more depth of characterization, more genuine emotional interplay than in earlier Japanese fiction. Tsubouchi has succeeded in terms of degree if not in kind.

The absence of any important studies of Tsubouchi's other fiction has been an even more serious deficiency in the critical literature. *Imotose kagami* resembles far more the novel Tsubouchi describes in his critical writing and must be so recognized. Tsubouchi has done a striking job in creating his hero Tatsuzō in spite of or perhaps because of the affinity the author himself felt to the story. The novel suffers from some severe imperfections—primarily those associated with the imbalance between the Tatsuzō-Otsuji marriage and the liaison between Tanuma Saikitsu and Oyuki—but the interplay between Tatsuzō and his wife is quite remarkable. His neglect of her, his despair with his own stupid choice, the selfishness that encircles and submerges his selfless instincts—all are extremely realistic, if by that term we mean a situation in which the reader can believe. Otsuji is stupid, sloppy, unattractive after her marriage in many ways, but we are deeply moved by her helplessness. She is a young woman stripped of every possible function, left to sit day by day in a hostile environment with absolutely nothing to do. She cannot help but win the reader's sympathy as much for her unattractive qualities as for the fact that she is so put upon by life at the very time she thought she would be happiest. This is precisely the "delving into the hearts of men" Tsubouchi had called for in *Shōsetsu shinzui*, and he is delving most successfully.

Matsu no uchi demonstrates how fragile a thing literary understanding can be. It is difficult to imagine that an author who had come as far toward his goal as Tsubouchi had in *Imotose kagami* could produce such a banal work, but produce it he did. Here the superficial in Tsubouchi won out over the more profound; apparently he thought to naturalize Western ideas with Japanese humor. He was groping for a way to narrow the dimensions of his plot, obviously in an attempt to develop individual characters more thoroughly. Although Tsubouchi never said that this kind of concentration on individuals is what makes a successful modern novel, he obviously came to think so as he wrote and talked with Futabatei. This essential point—limitation of plot, and number and variety of characters, in other words, the encapsulation of the human dilemma within the story of one or two people—was of the greatest influence on twentieth-century Japanese writers. Once this point was made clear the whole tone for Japanese fiction was set. For better or worse, the majority of later writers used an extremely limited cast of characters—often themselves—in a curtailed environment, seeing the microcosm as perhaps the only way of picturing the emotional world accurately.

Saikun was Tsubouchi's final expression of this concept and it is an admirable little book. Here he has replaced the foolish misunderstanding that weakened *Matsu no uchi* with an important set of conflicts. We are moved by the pathetic trust of the maid Osono, contrasted as it is with the selfishness of her mistress, who is so wretchedly treated in turn by her highly respected, indeed famous, husband. The interplay among the three characters is skillfully handled, each impinging for the briefest span of time on the other with the most telling results.

Tsubouchi was struggling to create a new fiction for Japan that would be as good as that of the West but that would be relevant to Japan. This obviously involved his reaching an understanding of the constituent elements of the novel, and he had to work for several years to develop this understanding. When he wrote *Shōsetsu shinzui* he was far from having grasped all the ideas that could be obtained from the novels he was reading, but perhaps no further than many contemporary critics of the Western world. In any case, it is foolish to assume he had worked out all the principles he needed or that he would even be able to use all he did understand in his first novel. A fair assessment of Tsubouchi as a novelist requires us to know all his fiction for only then does it become apparent that he was capable of writing a fine piece of realistic fiction as he had originally hoped.

Literary historians have further failed to see the significance of Tsubouchi's novels as social documents. There is no question that he recognized the degree of imbalance in the lives of men and women in Japan, and that he was seeking to expose it to the world at large. Concentrating as they have on the frivolousness of much of *Tōsei shosei katagi*, critics have not even noticed how frequently Tsubouchi dealt with this theme, and how much space he devoted to it. Substantial portions of *Tōsei shosei katagi*, and virtually all of *Imotose katagi* and *Saikun* are concerned with the victimization of women, as is another of his realistic novels that we did not analyze. It was a major concern of Tsubouchi's and it is surely significant that one of his poorer stories—*Matsu no uchi*—makes virtually no use of this theme.

We can learn a great deal about Meiji society from his novels, highly fictionalized though they were. Each of the stories is impregnated with the assumptions on which the society functioned, and the world Tsubouchi depicts is not far from the reality of contemporary life. The author presents in almost unvarnished fashion such aspects of the society as the romanticism permitted men by the licensed quarter, the rigidity of the class structure, the sternness of the traditional ethical code with its complex system of obligations and its insistence on ceaseless labor and self-improvement, and the pettiness and narrow confines of the lives of members of his own class. We furthermore clearly see the limitations of even the "best" minds of the period, comfortable as men were with the privileges they had inherited from the past and gained afresh in the modern world. What Tsubouchi is saying is that men do not change essentially, that what motivates the father may well motivate the son, despite the outward changes society may undergo.

More important to Tsubouchi the novelist, as distinct from his role of social observer, was his awareness of the basic egocentricity of the human experience. He had already begun to hint at this in *Tōsei shosei katagi* but it is not fully expressed until *Imotose kagami* where the main structure of the novel is built around this conception. And finally in *Saikun*, brief though it is, he has gone beyond the more obvious man-woman dichotomy to describe the isolation of one human being from another and man's inhumanity to man.

In four years Tsubouchi had dramatically refined his novelistic technique and in the end had produced a finely honed story in the modern mode. The solutions he reached with such effort became the formula for Japanese writers from the first decade of the twentieth century on. Although Tsubouchi never wrote of himself, he wrote constantly of what he might have been, that is, of some fictional being whose life style was sufficiently similar to his own to be readily identifiable. He was of course writing of the only people he knew well, but he was a student of fiction and never considered the possibility of autobiography. Authors of the twentieth century have taken the additional step of writing often entirely about their own experiences. Their canvas too is small, indeed almost confined, and their use of drama, as we have said, often nonexistent. Characteristically the fiction of twentieth-century Japan is a thinly disguised recounting of the author's own life, interesting or dull though it may be. The world of this fiction is inhabited by isolated human beings who barely interact with other people. In this sense, *Saikun* anticipates much of what we have come to think of as modern Japanese fiction, although it shows far more invention and a greater sense of dramatic tension than many of its successors.

Bibliography

An annotated bibliography of works by Tsubouchi is included in the *Shōyō senshū*, vol. 3 of the *Bessatsu*. Although published in 1927, it is still a useful guide to his earlier works. It was prepared in close consultation with the author, as was the entire fourteen volume collection. In using the bibliography, caution is necessary regarding dates of publication and possible omissions in the listings as some errors have been found.

The four novels analyzed in this study appear in the *Shōyō senshū*, vol. 1 of the *Bessatsu*. *Kokoya kashiko* and *Tanehiroi*, Tsubouchi's two other realistic novels, were not included in the collection. They may be read in the newspapers in which they were first printed, which are still extant. *Kokoya kashiko* was reprinted in a separate volume in 1956 by the Waseda Daigaku Kokubun Gakkai. *Tōsei shosei katagi* has appeared in many editions and most recently has been reprinted in *Tsubouchi Shōyō shū*, edited by Inagaki Tatsurō, vol. 16 in the series *Meiji bungaku zenshū* (Tokyo: Chikuma Shobō, 1969). *Imotose kagami* also appears in this volume.

An excellent chronological bibliography of secondary studies relating to Tsubouchi and his work is included in the *Tsubouchi Shōyō shū* edited by Inagaki.

Works Cited in this Study

Fukuchi Gen'ichirō. "Harunoya Shujin no *Saikun*." *Kokumin no tomo*, no. 39 (January 1889), p. 32.
A contemporary review of Tsubouchi's last novel.

Ichijima Shunjō. "Meiji bungaku shoki no tsuioku." *Shōsetsu shinzui*. In *Meiji bungaku meicho zenshū*. Tokyo: Tōkyōdō, 1926.
Recollections of Tokyo life in the early Meiji by a contemporary. The article is included in a collection of notable works of the Meiji period.

Inagaki Tatsurō. "Kaidai." *Tsubouchi Shōyō shū*. In *Meiji bungaku zenshū*, 16 : 388–400. Tokyo: Chikuma Shobō, 1969.
A critical analysis of Tsubouchi's work by the editor of this volume.

Ishibashi Ningetsu. "*Nisegane tsukai, Matsu no uchi*." *Kokumin no tomo*, no. 31 (October 1888), pp. 38–39.
A contemporary review by a well-known Meiji critic of *Matsu no uchi*.

Kawatake Shigetoshi. *Ningen Tsubouchi Shōyō*. Tokyo: Shinjusha, 1959.
A rather disjointed series of pieces on Tsubouchi by one of his best known disciples.

———— and Yanagida Izumi. *Tsubouchi Shōyō*. Tokyo: Fuzanbō, 1939.
The definitive biography of Tsubouchi by two of his disciples. It contains an extensive array of useful material, but is careful not to tarnish the reputation of its subject.

Kōjiro Tanesuke. "*Tōsei shosei katagi* kadai." *Tōsei shosei katagi*. In *Meiji bungaku meicho zenshū*, pp. 1–15. Tokyo: Tōkyōdō, 1926.
A discussion of Tsubouchi's first novel that quotes reviews that appeared when the novel was originally published.

Nakamura Mitsuo. *Futabatei Shimei den*. Tokyo: Kōdansha, 1958.
An intelligent and challenging biography of Futabatei by one of Japan's leading literary critics.

Ryan, Marleigh. *Japan's First Modern Novel*. New York: Columbia University Press, 1967.
A critical biography of Futabatei Shimei and translation of his novel *Ukigumo*.

Takada Sanae. "*Tōsei shosei katagi* no hihyō." *Gendai bungakuron taikei*. 1:9–18. Edited by Nakashima Kenzō and Yoshida Seiichi. 3rd printing. Tokyo: Kawade Shobō, 1960.
The most famous contemporary review of Tsubouchi's first novel reprinted in an anthology of criticism.

Tsubouchi Shikō. *Tsubouchi Shōyō kenkyū*. Tokyo: Waseda Bungaku Shuppanbu, 1953.
A somewhat helpful but very limited set of biographical essays by Tsubouchi's nephew and heir.

Tsubouchi Shōyō. "Kai randan." *Shōsetsu shinzui*. In *Meiji bungaku meicho zenshū*, pp. 162–72. Tokyo: Tōkyōdō, 1926.
The author's own account of his university days and early literary experiences.

———. *Shōyō senshū*. Tokyo: Shun'yōdō, 1927.
The largest collection of Tsubouchi's works available. It is printed with the original orthography and diacritical marks, making it of far greater value than later edited versions. Many of the plates from the original editions are included, and all prefaces and other apparatus are reproduced.

Wada Shigejirō. "Shōyō *Imotose kagami* shiron." *Ritsumeikan bungaku* (January 1958), pp. 1–13.
A brief and rather superficial critical essay on *Imotose kagami*.

Yanagida Izumi. "Tsubouchi sensei to josei." *Meiji Taishō bungaku kenkyū*, no. 16 (1955), pp. 64–70.
A defense of Tsubouchi's relations with women written by

his disciple and biographer in response to some scurrilous articles that had appeared in the early 1950s about Tsubouchi's marriage.

———. *Wakaki Tsubouchi Shōyō*. Tokyo: Shunjūsha, 1960. Using many of the techniques of Western scholarship, Yanagida here attempts an exhaustive biography of Tsubouchi's early years. The study is limited by the author's reticence to say anything that might offend the memory of his subject, but it contains an enormous amount of detail.

Yoda Gakkai. "Harunoya-kun shōsetsu *Saikun*." *Kokumin no tomo*, no. 41 (February 1889), pp. 22–26.
A contemporary review of Tsubouchi's last novel.

Index

Publications on Asia of the
Institute for Comparative and Foreign Area Studies

1. Compton, Boyd (trans. and ed.). *Mao's China: Party Reform Documents, 1942–44.* 1952. Reissued 1966. Washington Paperback–4, 1966. 330 pp., map.
2. Chiang, Siang-tseh. *The Nien Rebellion.* 1954. 177 pp., bibliog., index, maps.
3. Chang, Chung-li. *The Chinese Gentry: Studies on Their Role in Nineteenth-Century Chinese Society.* Introduction by Franz Michael. 1955. Reissued 1967. Washington Paperback on Russia and Asia–4. 277 pp., bibliog., index, tables.
4. *Guide to the Memorials of Seven Leading Officials of Nineteenth-Century China.* Summaries and indexes of memorials to Hu Lin-i, Tseng Kuo-fan, Tso Tsung-tang, Kuo Sung-tao, Tseng Kuo-ch'üan, Li Hung-chang, Chang Chih-tung, 1955. 457 pp., mimeographed. Out of print.
5. Raeff, Marc. *Siberia and the Reforms of 1822.* 1956. 228 pp., maps, bibliog., index. Out of print.
6. Li Chi. *The Beginnings of Chinese Civilization: Three Lectures Illustrated with Finds at Anyang.* 1957. Reissued 1968. Washington Paperback on Russia and Asia–6. 141 pp., illus., bibliog., index.
7. Carrasco, Pedro. *Land and Polity in Tibet.* 1959. 318 pp., maps, bibliog., index.

8. Hsiao, Kung-chuan. *Rural China: Imperial Control in the Nineteenth Century*. 1960. Reissued 1967. Washington Paperback on Russia and Asia–3. 797 pp., illus., bibliog., index.
9. Hsiao, Tso-liang. *Power Relations within the Chinese Communist Movement, 1930–34*. Vol I: *A Study of Documents*. 1961. 416 pp., bibliog., index, glossary. Vol. II: *The Chinese Documents*. 1967. 856 pp.
10. Chang, Chung-li. *The Income of the Chinese Gentry*. Introduction by Franz Michael. 1962. 387 pp., tables, bibliog., index.
11. Maki, John M. *Court and Constitution in Japan: Selected Supreme Court Decisions, 1948–60*. 1964. 491 pp., bibliog., index.
12. Poppe, Nicholas, Leon Hurvitz, and Hidehiro Okada. *Catalogue of the Manchu-Mongol Section of the Toyo Bunko*. 1964. 391 pp., index.
13. Spector, Stanley. *Li Hung-chang and the Huai Army: A Study in Nineteenth-Century Chinese Regionalism*. Introduction by Franz Michael. 1964. 399 pp., maps, tables, bibliog., glossary, index.
14. Michael, Franz and Chung-li Chang. *The Taiping Rebellion: History and Documents*. Vol I: *History*. 1966. 256 pp., maps, index. Vols. II and III: *Documents and Comments*. 1971. 1,107 pp.
15. Shih, Vincent Y. C. *The Taiping Ideology: Its Sources, Interpretations, and Influences*. 1967. 567 pp., bibliog., index.
16. Poppe, Nicholas. *The Twelve Deeds of Buddha: A Mongolian Version of the Lalitavistara; Mongolian Text, Notes, and English Translation*. 1967. 241 pp., illus. Paper.
17. Hsia, Tsi-an. *The Gate of Darkness: Studies on the Leftist Literary Movement in China*. Preface by Franz Michael. Introduction by C. T. Hsia. 1968. 298 pp., index.

18. Hsiao, Tso-liang. *The Land Revolution in China, 1930–1934: A Study of Documents*. 1969. 376 pp., tables, glossary, bibliog., index.
19. Gasster, Michael. *Chinese Intellectuals and the Revolution of 1911: The Birth of Modern Chinese Radicalism*. 1969. 320 pp., glossary, bibliog., index.
20. Thornton, Richard C. *The Comintern and the Chinese Communists, 1928–31*. 1969. 266 pp., index.
21. Lin, Julia C. *Modern Chinese Poetry: An Introduction*. 1972. 278 pp.
22. Huang, Philip C. *Liang Ch'i-ch'ao and Modern Chinese Liberalism*. 1972. 200 pp., illus., index.
23. Gerow, Edwin and Margery Lang, eds. *Studies in the Language and Culture of South Asia*. 1974. 174 pp.
24. Morrison, Barrie M. *Lalmai, A Cultural Center of Early Bengal*. 1974. 190 pp., maps, drawings, tables.
25. Hsiao, Kung-chuan. *A Modern China and a New World. K'ang Yu-Wei, Reformer and Utopian, 1858–1927*. Transliteration table, bibliog., index. Forthcoming, 1975.
26. Ryan, Marleigh Grayer. *The Development of Realism in the Fiction of Tsubouchi Shōyō*. 1975. 126 pp., index.
27. Suh, Dae-Sook and Chae-Jin Lee, eds. *Political Leadership in Korea*. Forthcoming, 1975.